Praise for *Heaven Has Blue Carpet*

Sharon's title, *Heaven Has Blue Carpet*, intrigued me. I thought, "What in the world is this about?" When I read she and the family chose to leave city life for farm life, which was ultimately devoted to sheep rearing, I thought, "No way!" But I went from horror to joy about her decision. I found myself utterly charmed as she shared her personal new insights about the old metaphor of the shepherd and the sheep. Not only was I charmed as I related her story, I learned a few things: sheep need occasional "flushing." Who knew?

> —Marilyn Meberg, Women of Faith
> speaker and author of *Love Me . . .*
> *Never Leave Me*

If I had to summarize this fascinating and spell-binding book, I would simply say that this is one of godly doctrine and expressive thought by someone who is one of God's brilliant shepherdesses. The concept of being taught lessons learned from raising sheep is unique. The concepts that can help you have a better relationship with Jesus, the Master Shepherd, will prepare the pasture of our hearts for fertile relationships with the Good Shepherd. Snuggle under the warmth of a wool blanket or with a cup of tea and learn more about the Lamb of God who takes away the sin of the world. You are certain to walk through the green pastures of life more confidently and comfortably.

> —Dr. Thelma Wells, president of A
> Woman of God Ministries, speaker,
> author, and mentor

I love this book! It is laugh-out-loud funny and yet profound and refreshing in its insight. Sharon gifts us with a new understanding of how tenderly our Father shepherds his children.

—Sheila Walsh, Women of Faith speaker
and author of *Get Off Your Knees and Pray*

Imagine James Herriot come back to life as a suburban housewife who knows nothing about sheep until she starts to raise some of her own. Imagine Herriot's sparkling eye and homespun humor discovering the indignities and glories of sheep for the first time, poignantly and hilariously. You've imagined Sharon Niedzinski.

—Ken Wilson, pastor and author of
*Jesus Brand Spirituality: He Wants
His Religion Back*

HEAVEN HAS
BLUE CARPET

A Sheep Story
by a Suburban Housewife

SHARON STARK
NIEDZINSKI

THOMAS NELSON
Since 1798

NASHVILLE   DALLAS   MEXICO CITY   RIO DE JANEIRO   BEIJING

Published in Nashville, Tennessee, by Thomas Nelson. Thomas Nelson is a registered trademark of Thomas Nelson, Inc.

Thomas Nelson, Inc. titles may be purchased in bulk for educational, business, fundraising, or sales promotional use. For information, please e-mail SpecialMarkets@thomasnelson.com.

Scripture quotations, unless otherwise indicated, are taken from the Holy Bible, New International Version (NIV). © 1973, 1978, 1984. International Bible Society. Used by permission of Zondervan Bible Publishers.

The Message by Eugene H. Peterson. © 1993, 1994, 1995, 1996, 2000. Used by permission of NavPress Publishing Group. All rights reserved.

THE AMPLIFIED BIBLE: OLD TESTAMENT. ©1962, 1964 by Zondervan (used by permission); and from THE AMPLIFIED BIBLE: NEW TESTAMENT. © 1958 by the Lockman Foundation (used by permission).

The Living Bible. © 1971. Used by permission of Tyndale House Publishers, Inc., Wheaton, Illinois 60189. All rights reserved.

THE CONTEMPORARY ENGLISH VERSION. © 1991 by the American Bible Society. Used by permission.

Library of Congress Cataloging-in-Publication Data

Niedzinski, Sharon Stark.
    Heaven has blue carpet : a sheep story by a suburban housewife / Sharon Stark Niedzinski.
        p. cm.
    ISBN 978-0-8499-2004-2 (trade paper)
    1. Discipling (Christianity) 2. Sheep—Religious aspects—Christianity. 3. Spiritual formation. I. Title.
BV4520.N49 2008
242—dc22
                            2008012155

Printed in the United States of America

08 09 10 11 12 RRD 5 4 3 2 1

I would like to dedicate this book to our twenty-one grandchildren . . .
our most beautiful lambs.

Ryan and Lauren Niedzinski
Nicole, Michelle, Andrew, and Rebecca Young
Nathan, Brandon, Jason, and Amy Sklenar
Adam, Andrea, Austin, and Abby Marthaler
Amanda, Emily, Allison, Samantha, and Ethan Ulstad
Grant and Kate Niedzinski

"The secret things belong to the LORD our God,
but the things revealed belong to us and to our children, forever,
that we may follow all the words of this law."
(Deut. 29:29)

"Know that the LORD is God. It is he who made us,
and we are his; we are his people, the sheep of his pasture."
Psalm 100:3

Have You Been Snipped, Dipped, Clipped, and Sheared?
Adopted, Adored, Taught, and Restored?
Then you are a sheep of his pasture.

CONTENTS

INTRODUCTION

I was living the predictable life of a suburban housewife and mother of six when my husband and I left our beautiful neighborhood and moved to a dilapidated centennial farm in the country. My husband and kids were excited to finally have their boarded horses in their backyard, while I had all I could do to keep on top of sump pumps, strange farm varmints, and all the muddy boots, shoes, and jeans piled up by the back door. Would you believe I planted my first vegetable garden on a lush pasture only plowed up once? It was a fifty-by-one-hundred foot nightmarish jungle (in pre-Roundup days). My husband parked his huge trailer next to this monstrous garden for my continuous weeding that painful first summer. I was definitely a genuine greenhorn!

So how did I end up with sheep? While I was fixing up the house, I looked at the green, rolling pasture, and a new theme emerged: "New England Countryside." So I ordered a flock of white Columbia ewes to match the Waverly blue-plaid wallpaper, matching curtains, and blue carpet in the house. Little did I know what I was in for!

Looking back, I can see it was entirely the Lord's idea for me to get those sheep. But of course, I didn't know it at the time. I had been asking the Lord how I could better know, hear, and follow him in my Christian walk. Well, he answered me—but who would ever have imagined in a trillion years that he would answer me allegorically, as I, this suburban housewife, raised a flock of sheep! While dealing with orphaned lambs, tail cuttings, and foot rot, I began to experience firsthand the amazing truths buried in the hundreds of Scriptures referencing God as our Shepherd and us as his sheep. These truths radically changed my life and brought me into the presence of our hardworking, sweat-stained, real-life Shepherd—Jesus, Son of God.

Through my sixteen years of shepherding, I discovered many

significant and crucial reasons why God chose the sheep/shepherd relationship as an analogy for his relationship with us, the secrets of which have unfortunately been slowly forgotten as the world has modernized. I pray God will use these allegorical stories to give you these pertinent truths and revolutionize your relationship with him as your Shepherd. This lost understanding that God is our Shepherd and we are his sheep is more important to grasp now than ever before.

With the intense pace of life today, most of us must dog paddle nonstop just to stay afloat. Today, people are struggling to integrate their marriages, money, careers, and Jesus into their overstuffed schedules. Parents of children are dealing with BlackBerrys and iPods, soccer and hockey on Sunday mornings, and practices and homework every day of the week. They are driving their young children and teens to weekend games (many out of state), multiple summer camps (to ensure acceptance on the better team), and paying for tutors. These kids are trying so hard to gain acceptance and applause that thousands are resorting to self-destructive behaviors such as drug and alcohol abuse, cutting, and eating disorders. And did I mention sex?

People the world over believe they can find happiness and fulfillment by pursuing the world's pleasures, goods, and acclaim. And yet millions are disillusioned, empty, and desolate.

Ah, but the Good Shepherd has such a different plan for us bamboozled sheep! I'm excited for you, the reader, to internalize in a whole new way the relationship between a sheep and his shepherd, and the resulting acceptance and fulfillment mankind was born to have! I pray you will be entertained, bestirred, and inspired as you walk alongside this greenhorn shepherd on her crazy journey into Sheep World. Enjoy!

> "My sheep listen to my voice; I know them, and they
> follow me. I give them eternal life, and they shall
> never perish; no one can snatch them out of my hand."
> John 10:27–28

FOREWORD

"Hello, Sharon? This is Karen, your Realtor. I've just looked at an old turn-of-the-century farm that will be going on the market tomorrow. I think you and Ron should take a look at it."

Look at it? It's been three years since I've heard from her.

"As soon as I saw the property, I thought of your family. It's exactly what you and Ron were looking for but never found. You'd better get there quick."

She sounds out of breath. I can't believe this. I was sure she had written us off as a couple of dreamers looking for a pie-in-the-sky farm that doesn't exist. Well, not on our budget anyhow.

"What's the address?"

"Honey, let's not even look at it. I don't want to move, no matter how nice it is. Jerry is graduating from high school in a few months, the four girls love it here, and we have a new baby. Let's face it. This opportunity has come too late, and we're too old for a farm."

"I agree. It sounds like too much work."

But neither of us could resist. We just wanted a peek.

With the North Thomas Road address in Freeland, Michigan, scribbled on a napkin, we took off. We were familiar with Freeland. Every fall my husband (Honey) and I took the kids to Bintz's Apple Mountain for their mouthwatering caramel apples, warm powdered-sugar doughnuts, and cold cider. We loved the cider mill. Every year they'd have to tell us to leave so other people could get in . . . we were perennially captivated by the noisy crushing and grinding of apples and bumblebees. We did have happy feelings about Freeland. *Hmmm.*

Leaving the busy five-lane road, we turned left, drove over the Tittabawassee River and continued west, almost missing North Thomas Road. It wasn't paved.

"Honey, where did this road come from? We've gone right by here for years."

North Thomas Road was a winding sandy road bordered on both sides with full-growth woods. The huge old trees gracefully covered the road like a canopy. It was so beautiful that tears came to my eyes. Then we caught sight of what looked like an old homestead.

"Honey, look, our favorite tree."

A large, mature stand of Michigan white pines greeted us. Before we had even sighted the farmhouse, we knew something was up.

"Is your heart pounding?"

"Yes."

"Mine is too."

Then we beheld the old Saginaw brick and fieldstone farmhouse with its wraparound porch, and all kinds and sizes of long-vacated outbuildings. I took in a deep breath, as if I could literally take it all in, and then it seemed I exhaled, as though, finally, I was home.

Honey must have experienced something similar as he broke the silence by whispering, "This is it."

I whispered back, "I know."

"We have to do it."

"I know we do."

"Oh my gosh! Look at that old barn. The kids will love it!"

Discussion about purchasing the homestead was unnecessary. We just knew this was it, our new home, and we hadn't even left the car.

To the back left of the farmhouse, behind the white pines, was a high ridge adorned with decades-old apple and pear trees. A big, old, red barn and silo loomed behind the house; half of it was sagging, but we excused it. To the back right of the house, the picture was fringed in row after row of well-tended grapes. We couldn't believe this peaceful, 1800s oasis existed in the middle of such an upscale, growing community. And we were delighted to discover this farm was the only dwelling on the whole two-mile, tree-lined, sandy road.

God had put rose-colored glasses on us, of course. When we

brought our children and our parents to see the new purchase, one of our children started crying, and both of our parents questioned our decision. Obviously, we were the only ones who got the glasses.

We sold our beautiful home in the suburbs, took our children out of their private school, took our two horses out of boarding, and moved in.

Our work had just begun. The home, barn, outbuildings, and pastures had been neglected for years. Hidden deep in the overgrowth were discarded scraps and parts of cars, tractors, tires, even an old, early sixties console television. Each discovery delighted the finder, and we saw all of our "finds" taken away several times by a very large rented dump truck. Only the vineyard was taken care of. We were to learn that the owner's three married sons planted and tended the multiple varieties of delicious grapes that covered almost a quarter of an acre. Their parents, the owners, were now living in Texas and wanted to sell.

A local excavator called us and offered to dig us a pond. Honey told him we didn't want a pond; neither did our funds allow for such amenities. He called every few days, lowering the price. When the kids heard about these discussions, they began mentally adding a raft, a dock, and a rowboat to the preposterous picture. Honey and I could only envision a large, dry hole, because as far as we knew, the property was sand based. We continued to say no.

Weeks of phone calls passed. Finally exhausted, the excavator said he would dig the pond for free if he could just have all the sand. He explained he was just starting out in his business, and he needed the sand for a big job coming up.

It had been obvious our Master Contractor had been sending us Christian men to help us remodel the house . . . and so to resolve this new dilemma, Honey told the kids, "If this guy is a Christian man, I'll be open to discussing this whole pond idea with him."

The kids were jumping and clapping and hugging Dad as if everything was settled. Dad looked a bit quizzical for a moment, and then he called the excavator.

We were to meet the mysterious excavator at the farm after dinner. We waited for him on the old wraparound porch. It was a hot night. The kids were as excited as if it were Christmas Eve. We, however, were suspicious.

He finally drove up in a battered, noisy old truck. He turned the ignition off. I can still remember the silence . . . I think everyone stopped breathing. Out stepped a lanky young man with long, unruly, blond hair, wearing only cowboy boots, blue jeans, and a huge gold cross on his sweaty, bared chest.

"Are you a Christian?" I asked him right off, hoping to disguise my first impression.

"Yes I am, praise the Lord!"

He said it unashamedly, with a grin larger than life.

The applause coming from the porch stunned him. The blow to my ungodly discernment hit hard but fair.

The excavator began digging a teardrop-shaped pond to the north of the house. He kept digging and digging for sand that never came. He finally stopped at a depth of thirty feet, when three natural springs were uncovered. We now had a thirty-foot-deep adobe clay, spring-fed pond. This deep clay container held the fresh water like a poured cement pool . . . a perfect swimming pond. Everyone was shocked except the kids; every area of the farm was sand based, except that to the north of the house.

We soon allowed our disillusioned excavator to haul away sand from the high ridge behind the house, which turned that ridge into a beautiful rolling pasture, perfect for . . . something.

part one

THE FIRST YEAR

chapter one

A RAM IS COMING!

They were sending us a ram. It never occurred to me, when I pictured living on a farm with split-rail fencing and rolling pastures, polka-dotted with grazing sheep, that I'd ever need a ram. The previous owners had never mentioned a ram when they sold us the place.

A ram? What would I do with a ram? Well, that was the silly question of the year. I *am* the mother of six children. But you don't just open the crate and say, "Hello, ram. Come and meet our sheep." There's a lot more to it than that, especially when you were not raised on a farm and don't know squat about raising sheep.

"Honey, the ram will be here any minute. Tell me, why did I choose to get sheep? I'm already raising a flock of kids!"

Honey laughed. I could only shake my head. *What have I gotten myself into?*

It was a beautiful, sunny June morning. With a big smile I announced to the family that the sheep man would be delivering our sheep any minute. No one knew I had a blizzard of berserk butterflies in my stomach that wouldn't stop flittering around. I skipped breakfast. I had spent the night caught in a fitful and fearful nightmare about the ominous coming winter. Before I fell asleep I was thinking about the last thing the sheep man said to me, "Don't worry; the sheep will be just fine on your pasture all summer." And then he left so quickly I didn't have to time to ask him what happens after summer.

The huge trailer drove up the long drive to the barn.

"Kids, can you hear them? They're baa-ing hello."

"Mom, give us a break!"

The sheep man drove the trailer through the double gate into our newly fenced pasture, fumbled with the trailer latch, and slid the door open.

"Just got your mamas sheared for you!"

He said it in such a way that I responded with a "thank you," but I hadn't comprehended what he said until I saw them. Spilling out of that trailer was a whole bunch of bald sheep with oversized pink udders bouncing so violently I was afraid their weight would make them detach. These creatures didn't even look like sheep!

I wiped the tears from my eyes before my family would notice.

These bare-naked sheep were hyper and excitable; not at all like I imagined. I didn't know they had never been on a pasture before and the only thing they had ever eaten was dry hay. Our mouths dropped as we watched these deformed-looking sheep overzealously tearing at their first taste of grass; now in one spot, and then another, until they all had so much grass stuffed in their mouths that they couldn't chew or swallow. Then some of them tried and started gagging.

No one in the family said a word. We just stared. As the sheep spread across the pasture, I worried they would munch down the whole field in one day. I was sure I'd ordered too many sheep.

"Good luck with the sheep! Let us know if you need anything. Oh, they've never been on grass before, so watch 'em. Don't keep 'em on it long." *Now he tells me.*

I heard the motor start up and saw him backing down the driveway. Not understanding what he had said, and realizing the sheep didn't come with operating instructions, I ran after him yelling, "Wait! Wait! Now what do I do?"

His perplexed, questioning look made me realize I was exposing my total ignorance of sheep. Assuming I had some sheep savvy, he rolled down the truck window.

"You can take 'em off the grass for a while if you want to. We just took their lambs away from them, so they'll be a little miserable for a day or two, and don't pay any attention to their bawling; their udders will eventually calm down.

"You took their lambs away?" *I didn't know they were mothers.*

"Well, they're not market ready yet, but we'll put the grain to them."

What was he talking about?

"What should I do with their udders?"

The truck screeched and stopped. Responding to my stupid question and, more likely, my stupid look, the sheep man opened the door a bit and yelled out again, only in a louder, slightly aggravated voice, "Don't worry about them! All they'll need for the next few months is a good pasture and water! Just let them graze and relax. They'll be fine; they'll be just fine!"

I stood there watching him drive down the driveway and then down the road.

When he was out of sight, I reluctantly turned my head and took a last look at my new project. Walking back to the house, I repeated over and over the only instructions I was given: "All they'll need is pasture and water, pasture and water. Relax, relax. They'll be fine; they'll be just fine."

I was relieved when the ewes lost their voices after bleating and bawling for their lambs nonstop for a week . . . and my family started sleeping again. And the sheep started to look semi-acceptable to me when their zany-looking udders began to shrink and the fuzzy beginnings of wool emerged and covered their unclothed bodies.

But I didn't stop worrying until their bright-green baseball-size doo-doos turned back into dry little pebbles and our new pasture no longer looked like a waste dump.

One morning I noticed that everyone in the family was making a special effort to check on the sheep through the kitchen window.

"Look, a group of them are at the top of the hill under the old apple trees."

"Mom, don't they look pretty grazing up there?"

"Uh-oh, they're eating the fallen apples. Will apples hurt them?"

The scene set before us was both tranquil and thrilling as our once-unnoticed pasture was now an animated pastoral landscape with possible dangers and delights. Plus . . . it was the perfect decor—it definitely matched the wallpaper and was definitely New England Countryside. They were doing "just fine in the pasture all summer."

I had two blissful months into my new project when . . .

"Hi! This is the wife of the man you bought your sheep from. We'll be dropping off our old ram, Moses, for you to use around the first of September."

"Pardon me?"

"You know, John says you can borrow our ram this year. You know, until you can get your own."

"My own? A ram?"

"We could pick one up for you at Saturday's auction if you're not fussy."

"No, no, yours will be fine. When did you say it will be coming? In September?"

Shocked and confused, I didn't even thank her for their generous offer. It was then I realized I had been deposited into an alien world where the inhabitants, their language, and their game plan were completely foreign to me. Thankfully I had subscribed to two sheep magazines. One was called *sheep!* and the other, *Shepherd.* I frantically picked up one and then the other, thumbing through every page, looking for the word *ram*, while praying, "Oh God, please . . . let there be something in here about rams . . . anything!" There was, and I whispered a heartfelt "Thank you," but I couldn't decipher the instructions.

The article said to "flush" the ewes two weeks before you turn the ram in. I turned those magazines inside and out but couldn't find one clue on what it meant to "flush a ewe." I knew one thing for sure . . . I didn't like the sound of the word *flush*.

My brainless motivation for purchasing sheep was now exposed, and I was ashamed. I was sure I would have to flush out their udders or something even more disgusting for my penance. I decided that day I had better get with the program and start studying about these mysterious creatures eating our grass.

I started a study of sheep that ended up lasting all the years I raised them. I eventually covered sheep genetics, reproduction, health, nutrition, and marketing. I attended sheep conventions, auctions, and county fairs. I even visited a slaughterhouse. But it would take years of applying what I had learned and a changed heart before I could call myself a "shepherd of sheep."

> Then I will give you shepherds after my own heart, who will lead
> you with knowledge and understanding. (Jeremiah 3:15)

But on this day, I would have to find someone who knew what "flushing" meant.

chapter two

WHAT IS "FLUSHING"?

I was waiting at the barn door of the largest sheep operation in our state. I had been delighted to learn it was only three miles from our farm and was informed that a farm only three miles away can be considered a close neighbor.

I wore the new shepherding clothes I had ordered from the Cabela's catalog; a pretty red barn coat with a brown leather collar and cool, all-weather rubber moccasin boots.

Because there wasn't a nameplate over any of the doors in the barn, I wasn't quite sure where to go. Then a young kid appeared, and he told me he would find someone.

"You will find 'someone'?" I asked. "I have a ten o'clock appointment with Milo."

The kid just looked at me and left. I hoped Milo had checked his day planner that morning.

I waited at the barn door long enough to find myself redecorating the place. In my imagination, the owner of this operation had paved the farm-implement parking area where I stood. He had marked off parking spaces with bright yellow lines and added oodles of potted geraniums and a shiny brass plate over one of the doors, reading "Farm Office."

I was trying to figure out how all the machines that were abandoned in the parking area could untangle themselves and miss the potholes when three old sheep men came through the door.

I had no idea which one of the three was Milo. They didn't say hello or apologize for being late. They just stood there, looking at me.

I guessed they were waiting for me to speak first. I felt uncomfortable. *Maybe I'm overdressed . . .*

"Hi! I live just three miles down the road. We're neighbors! Close neighbors! Which one of you is Milo?"

The man with the below-the-belly pants, held up by a pair of overstretched, worn suspenders, grinned from ear to ear. I reached out to shake his hand when he stepped back, wiped his hands on his pants, and shook his head from side to side. Then the other two men did the exact same thing, and all three of them just stood there silently, waiting for me to continue. I got the message. These old sheep men weren't into networking. I decided to talk real fast, skip the chitchat, and get to the point.

"I'm expecting a ram in a few weeks, and an article I read said to 'flush' the ewes fourteen days before you turn the ram in. What I'd like to know is, what does 'flush' mean?"

They just stared at me. I guessed these sheep men didn't read articles on sheep. They had been raising sheep for such a long time, they just *did* things. They didn't name what they did either. The little disheveled man with a large wad of something in his mouth spoke.

"Ain't never heard of 'flushing.'"

"What do you do a couple of weeks before you turn the ram in?" I asked.

All three men just stared at me. I guess they didn't do much, or it was so obvious they just couldn't put it into words. Smiley Milo finally spoke.

"If you bring in a ram every September or October, you're gonna git lambs."

The others looked to their spokesman and nodded with approval and a torrent of little comments gushed out.

"That's right, Milo."

"Put in a good ram, and you're gonna git good lambs."

"Yup, every September or October, when the weather is cooler . . . that'll do it! Just bring 'em in."

Then they all nodded with a "you're dismissed; you've got your answer" kind of look and sauntered back to do whatever it is old sheep men do.

I went to the library and did my homework (those were precomputer days). From what I could tell, *flushing* was about getting the ewes physically and emotionally ready to breed with the ram. The whole idea of raising sheep was to produce bunches of lambs. If I did things right, whatever those things were, our ewes would have multiple births. Every time the phrase "if I did things right" crossed my mind, my spine would tighten up, and I would get an instant headache.

If I did do things right, our ewes would have twins, triplets, or quads. I would later find out that a 200 percent crop of lambs—one in which every ewe birthed at least twins—was a desirable and feasible goal. If a ewe did not produce multiple lambs, it would have to be culled. Again, Webster's Dictionary informed me that the word *cull* refers to something rejected, inferior, and worthless. Sheep farmers are supposed to get rid of such sheep. They should be culled right away.

Chew on This

In Ezekiel 34, God judged the religious leaders (shepherds) who were so caught up with their own concerns and agendas that they neglected their people (flocks). Because their people were not producing good fruit, God would have to remove them from their office as shepherds and hold them responsible.

That was my first realization of the serious consequences of poor shepherding. If one of my ewes doesn't produce at least twins, she would have to be thrown out, and it would be entirely my fault!

I was now ready to get serious about my new shepherding job. I wrote out a four-step flushing plan and studied it.

FLUSHING

Step One: Kick the ewes out of their pasture and bring them into the barn. *(Find out how to get them out.)*

Step Two: Bring each ewe into a stall, bring her down to the floor, *(How?)* and give her a personal examination. Look for injuries, bugs, burrs, or worms, and treat her if needed. *(Find out how to treat these things.)*

Step Three: Check each ewe's feet for foot rot and trim her overgrown hooves. *(Study foot rot and buy one sharp knife.)*

Step Four: Put the trimmed and treated ewes in a new pasture, and start giving them a small amount of grain every day for fourteen days until the ram comes. *(Ask Honey to put in fencing around a new pasture, and find out what kind of grain sheep eat.)*

I studied, made phone calls to Milo, shopped, and encouraged Honey. Honey was working harder than I was . . . on my project! He put in a split-rail fence around a second pasture and installed an Australian electric fencing system onto it. The new pasture had virginal, pristine grass with a small stand of shade trees in one corner. Honey also built a feeding trough, piped in water, and brought in a shiny new water trough.

"Do your sheep know they're about to enter Sheep Heaven?"

"No, but I do! You're awesome!"

Flushing day arrived, and two inexperienced greenhorns entered the summer pasture for the first time.

"Jane, they're running from us! This time let's try to get behind them and push them into the barn!"

But they will never follow a stranger; in fact, they will run away from him because they do not recognize a stranger's voice. (John 10:5)

"Mom, it's not working! They're scattering all over the place!"

I was thankful our thirteen-year-old daughter, Jane, had volunteered to be my assistant flusher. Now there were two ignorant shepherds at work.

"Two sheep are heading for the barn door! Close in behind them! Run! Shut the door!"

We followed the two ewes into the barn and somehow managed to get one of them into the newly built sheep stall. The three of us just stood there for a few seconds, breathing heavily, looking at each other. I was not prepared for the petrified look in the eyes of this ewe. She made me feel like the enemy rather than the shepherd.

"Okay, Jane. Now we have to get her down on the floor so we can look her over."

This ewe didn't want anything to do with us. I was confused. I had assumed sheep were docile and would let us do whatever it was we had to do to them. Of course, what did I know? The closest I had ever been to sheep was reading the children's rhymes about Mary. Didn't her lamb follow her to school?

Jane and I chased the ewe all over the stall until we were exhausted. We were playing tag, and she was winning.

"Our sheep don't know us, Jane. Once they do, it will be a lot easier. But today, one way or another, we have to bring this sheep down! We'd better pray." I would later find a detailed article with pictures showing me how to set a sheep on its rump. I made a copy, had it plasticized, and carried it with me until I had it down pat.

We tried again. This time we went at it with a do-or-die determination, knowing God was helping us. We were astonished that we actually brought down that large ewe. We even managed to enjoy a few laughs in our astonishment. Then we made a plan. The plan was for the "wrestler" to catch her breath while the "trimmer" examined the ewe and trimmed the feet. We would then trade positions for the next ewe. I would be the first to exam and trim, as the shiny new shepherd's knife was in my pocket.

The deafening wail coming out of this panic-stricken ewe was unnerving, and I hadn't even touched her feet. Nothing felt right about this. Then her ear-splitting bawl increased in pitch to pain level, so I raised my voice several decibels above hers, and lo and behold, she shut up. I probably scared her speechless. Jane and I now had control of the situation again, as ridiculous as it was.

I trimmed her hooves while praying I wouldn't cut her, and then Jane let her get up. She bolted out of the barn like an escapee . . . screeching like a madwoman.

We sat there in the straw for a few minutes, listening to our pounding hearts and the ewe's faraway baas.

"Good thing we have fences, or she'd be running through town by now." We laughed.

"We can do this, Mom! This is fun!"

The second ewe reacted exactly as the first one . . . scared stiff. Jane trimmed her feet with much more ease and competence than I. She had been taking care of her horse's hooves every day . . . picking, painting, and sometimes trimming them. All our girls were relaxed and confident with animals.

The two of us continued until every ewe was examined, trimmed, and released. The reward of the day was releasing these petrified ewes into our idea of sheep heaven. We were dirty, sweaty, and sore, but the surprise was how good it felt. I think we even strutted as we walked back to the house to report to the family. We felt tough and capable. In the retelling, we experienced the euphoria of having done what seemed impossible.

After capturing, examining, and trimming every ewe; putting bandages on three cut fingers; taping one sore ankle; and using up a tube of BENGAY on my lower back; I realized this wasn't about raising sheep—it was about getting in shape. I now had a new respect for shepherds. They were right up there in my book with triathletes, tap dancers, and the cyclists from the Tour de France.

chapter three

SHEEP TRAITS

"Honey, look . . . they love their new pasture. Once I start giving them a little grain, they'll know for sure they died and went to sheep heaven."

I called the farmer who sold us the sheep and asked him what kind of grain he fed the sheep, and exactly how much *is* a small grain ration?

"I feed my sheep whatever grain we have too much of."

That was not an acceptable answer. I eventually found out I could purchase cracked corn mixed with sheep vitamins and minerals from the local grain elevator, and the ration would be on the bag. Now, this I understood. The grain elevator was now my second favorite store. Still holding first place was the local Farm & Fleet store.

I nonchalantly walked into the sheep pasture with my newly purchased bag of grain, humming softly, thinking how much fun this was going to be. *The sheep are going to love me for this.*

As I opened the bag, every ewe instantly perked up her head and opened her eyes really wide, as though startled. I hesitated for a moment. Then I poured the grain into the feeder. The second the grain hit the feeder, the whole flock of sheep stampeded toward me like a runaway train. I barely made it out of the target zone. I stood there, shaking. Then these "docile" ewes proceeded to inhale their grain with such vociferous gobbling, I thought they might all choke to death! Many of them were coughing and heaving. It was disgusting. I was appalled to see their gluttonous reaction to food.

This gorging of food proved to be a sheep trait that disgusted our entire family throughout the years we had them. Our family sadly came to understand that the only thing sheep really wanted was their grain, their grass, and their own lambs . . . and in that order. Yes, sheep are selfish gluttons. It was a disheartening truth we faced day in, day out. Sheep definitely have a hard time seeing beyond their plates!

> Those who live according to the sinful nature have their minds
> set on what that nature desires; but those who live in accordance
> with the Spirit have their minds set on what the Spirit desires.
> (Romans 8:5)

A few days later, I read in *sheep!* magazine that sheep of all ages will often die of an overeating disease called *enterotoxemia*. Their basic nature to indulge can cause a sudden release of a deadly toxin by the bacterium Clostridium perfringens, Type D, in their digestive tract. This powerful poison, or toxin, can cause death in just a few hours. It can happen so quickly that the shepherd wouldn't even know the sheep was sick. A variation of this bacterium can also cause hemorrhagic enterotoxemia (Type C).

Whoa! Sheep are prone to two deadly diseases as a result of gluttony! Gross. Sheep left alone, living according to their inherent urges, could die terrible deaths before their time.

> Their destiny is destruction, their god is their stomach, and
> their glory is in their shame. Their mind is on earthly things.
> (Philippians 3:19)

Chew on This

Left alone, living without moral guidance or restrictions, living according to our inherent urges, we also will destroy ourselves and our environment. God the Father, our Creator, knew this. That is why he sent his Son to earth . . . to show us how to live. His Son would be our Shepherd, and if we would follow him, he would lead us into an abundant life. Jesus, our Shepherd, is the Path; he is the Way; he is the Truth and the Life.

The thief comes only in order to steal and kill and destroy. I came that they may have and enjoy life, and have it in abundance (to the full, till it overflows). (John 10:10 AMP)

There isn't a cure for these gluttony-produced, fatal diseases, but there was a vaccination that we hoped would protect the sheep from contracting them. The lambs also needed a tetanus shot and a booster every year.

At that point I decided I would get a law enacted that would require sellers of sheep to include neck tags with detailed instructions for feeding, flushing, vaccinations, and all warnings, side effects, precautions, and drug interactions.

The downside to raising sheep was pouring into me like a muddy flood, and the truth was tempting me to bail out. Negative fact number one: sheep are totally dependent upon their shepherd. Sounds like all work to me. Two: they are stubborn and so consumed with self that they don't realize it, and continue to fight my efforts. Three: they will push and shove to be the first in line so they can get the most grain. Four: they are so greedy that they step in their own food and dirty it all up while trying to get more than their neighbor. Five: if one of the ewes got caught in the feeder, the others wouldn't think twice about trampling on top of her just to get the grain.

> Is it not enough for you to feed on the good pasture? Must you also trample the rest of your pasture with your feet? Is it not enough for you to drink clear water? Must you also muddy the rest with your feet? Must my flock feed on what you have trampled and drink what you have muddied with your feet? (Ezekiel 34:18–19)

I struggled to sandbag the negative facts about my sheep, but the truth was the truth, and it was ugly.

I told the Lord, "God, I don't think I like your sheep anymore . . . they're disgusting. You'll have to change my heart, or I won't be able to do this."

A little grimy residue was left in me after the flood subsided. I was again committed to my sheep, but lurking under the surface was this general disgust and anger with them. I was secretly mad at them for weeks and only doing for them what I had to do.

Then one morning it hit me. I wasn't mad at my sheep—I was mad at myself. I am just like my sheep! I saw my ugly independence, stubbornness, and selfishness. I too was ignoring my Shepherd and going my own way, down my own path, pushing and shoving to get the most and the best for myself. I cried out to God and asked him to forgive me and help me change.

Then I saw the Good Shepherd with newly washed eyes. He was right there with me in the pasture! I fell to my knees and sobbed. A peace and an assurance that all was well washed over me . . . and I felt incredibly loved. *He loves me, even though I am a filthy sheep!*

> I saw myself so stupid and so ignorant; I must seem like an animal to you, O God. But even so, you love me! You are holding my right hand! (Psalm 73:22 – 23 TLB)

I will sprinkle clean water on you, and you will be clean; I will cleanse you from all your impurities and from all your idols. I will give you a new heart and put a new spirit in you; I will remove from you your heart of stone and give you a heart of flesh . . . I will save you from all your uncleanness. (Ezekiel 36:25–26, 29a)

After forgiving myself, I found I wasn't mad at the sheep anymore, and with true concern for them, I ordered everything I needed to vaccinate.

Chew on This

If you're not dreaming of an extreme makeover, then you haven't comprehended who you are; neither have you seen the Shepherd.

The Shearing Shed

Are you always judging, critical, or angry at your fellow man? Your attitude is an exact copy of your attitude toward yourself. You need to accept yourself for who you are . . . a hypocritical, bullheaded, nincompoop sheep like the rest of us. And then forgive yourself and allow the Lord to love you. If you do, you'll soon be accepting, forgiving, and loving every nincompoop you run into. You'll not love them because of who they are, how they act, or what they've done, but because you are so loved by God that you can love in return.

~

Three of our six kids were available to help me vaccinate the ewes. Jill, Jane, Ann, and I arrived at the barn early one Saturday morning, with our arms full of newly purchased supplies, and carefully lined them up on top of the sheep partition. We had several bottles of the vaccine, bottles of peroxide and alcohol, a whole box of syringes, cotton balls, a steaming bowl of hot water, soap, and a nice pile of clean towels. We were set.

The girls and I decided to make a narrow walkway through the barn to force the sheep into a single line so they couldn't back up or turn around on us. We used the portable fences Honey had made for the lambing pens. When we finished securing the fences, we were beaming with satisfaction and confidence.

The girls brought a good number of ewes into this narrow walkway.

"We're ready here, Mom, and the ewes seem pretty relaxed about it all."

"Good. Good. This is working great."

I injected the first needle in the bottle of vaccination, drew in the required dose, and then lifted the needle up high and let out a trial squirt.

"Mom, you look like you know what you're doing."

"Of course I do. I've seen *ER*."

The girls quietly snickered. They knew I was edgy about injecting my first living creature with a needle.

I gently reached out with the needle to the first lucky sheep . . . and in one instant every ewe in the chute leaped straight up and over the four-foot-high fencing! All of our supplies and all of the sheep disappeared in a matter of a second. It was such a mess, such a failure, and it happened in a snap. We were stunned. Finally someone broke the silence.

"Ann! You actually caught that ewe in midair."

"Yes, but I only held her for a second and she was gone."

"You caught a ewe?"

"Annie Bananee . . . you caught a ewe? A huge ewe? You couldn't have!"

"But I did!"

"I saw it, Mom. She actually caught it!"

We broke out into hilarious laughter and couldn't stop. We fell in the straw and laughed for a long time. Maybe because our Anne, a little third grader, actually reached out and unbelievably caught a 150-pound ewe midair. Or was it because we were facing the most staggering, mishmash mess any of us had ever seen? We literally had to go through the haystack to find all the needles!

Who would figure that sheep could jump up and over a four-foot-high fence from a standing position? It was obvious we didn't know sheep, and they didn't know us. We did vaccinate our sheep, but not that day.

As I continued to interact with sheep, I discovered the incredible depth of their fear. Sheep have an inborn spirit of fear of just about everything. They fear strangers, the unknown, loud noises, soft noises, sudden movements, and sudden sounds. I had to face another downside to sheep . . . they are panicky, lily-livered, weak-kneed scaredy-cats through and through!

Whenever I maneuvered a sheep down on the floor, it would lie there motionless, with a fear so deep it would become as paralyzed. Once the sheep was immobile, I could do just about anything I needed to do . . . shots, shearing, or trimming. Sheep are misled, entrapped victims of fear. Fear has blinded them from the truth that they weigh a heck of a lot more than we do.

For God did not give us a spirit of timidity (of cowardice, of craven and cringing and fawning fear), but [He has given us a spirit] of power and of love and of calm and well-balanced mind and discipline and self-control. (2 Timothy 1:7 AMP)

Are not two sparrows sold for a penny? Yet not one of them will fall to the ground apart from the will of your Father. And even the very hairs of your head are all numbered. So don't be afraid; you are worth more than many sparrows. (Matthew 10:29–31)

When I am afraid, I will trust in you. (Psalm 56:3)

Chew on This

Fear can mislead and immobilize us when we make it more powerful than God. If we are looking at the situation or our own fear, we'll freeze and do nothing, blinded to the strength and power available to us from the Lord. With God, we are twice the size of what we fear.

I was starting to believe that my sheep were blind and stone deaf, because they never responded to me when I called them. They never even looked up to acknowledge my presence. They were completely oblivious to me.

When I needed the sheep to come, I would call out the nice names our family gave them . . . "Heidi! Pearl! Sarah! Come here, Mary!" No response. Then I would think up some crazy names to call them, just to keep myself from hitting them on their thick-skulled heads. "Heidi-Schmeidi! Pearl-the-Girl! Hairy-Mary!" Of course I never got a response. It wouldn't be long before I started calling them by their *real* names. "You brain-dead numbskulls, half-baked morons, thickheaded dimwits, fog-brained boneheads, dumbbell nincompoops, can't you hear me?!"

They didn't know I wanted to take them down the road to a new, lush pasture. They didn't know that if they stayed where they were, in their stubborn ignorance, they'd soon be licking dirt.

> Today, if you hear his voice, do not harden your hearts as you did in the rebellion, during the time of testing in the desert. (Hebrews 3:7-8)

I came to the conclusion that their bullheaded indifference to anyone except themselves was causing their deafness and blindness. I had to figure out how to crack their hard, selfish hearts. What would I have to do to . . . Become a sheep so I could talk sheep-talk?

> So come, let us worship: bow before him,
>   on your knees before God, who made us!
> Oh yes, he's our God,
>   and we're the people he pastures, the flock he feeds.
> Drop everything and listen, listen as he speaks:
>   "Don't turn a deaf ear as in the Bitter Uprising,
> As on the day of the Wilderness Test,
>   when your ancestors turned and put me to the test.
> For forty years they watched me at work among them,
>   as over and over they tried my patience.
> And I was provoked—oh, was I provoked!
>   'Can't they keep their minds on God for five minutes?
>   Do they simply refuse to walk down my road?'
> Exasperated, I exploded,
>   'They'll never get where they're headed, never be able to sit
>   down and rest.'" (Psalm 95:6–11 MSG)

The Shearing Shed

Father God, I acknowledge and renounce my selfishness, gluttony, fear, stubbornness, deafness, and blindness. Forgive me! Plow up the ground of my hard-hearted selfish heart and seed and water it with your Word and your Love. Open my eyes and ears . . . Give me a hunger and attentiveness to see you in my pasture and hear you call my name!

chapter four

MOSES CAME

Our ewes were as flushed as we could make them. Webster's definition of someone being flushed was right on. The ewes were glowing, overflowing with life and vigor, affluent, and lacked nothing.

We heard the sheep man and his wife drive up in their small pickup truck. The kids, my mother, and our two dogs arrived at the scene just as they drove through the gate into the pasture. They looked a little confused by the large audience and asked us why we were all there. We didn't want to tell them that we had never seen a ram up close before and that we had been working our fingers to the bone getting our ewes ready for this momentous occasion. So, in imitation of all good sheep people, we said nothing. We just smiled.

"Gotcha here a Suffolk, old Moses."

"A Suffolk? But our ewes are white Columbias."

"No different. He'll make good lambs."

"But . . . what color will our lambs be?"

"All different, ma'am; they'll be all different."

I can't believe it. I wanted all white lambs. And I never get a straight answer!

"You look a little serious there, ma'am. I know he's old, but don't you worry, he'll do his job; you can count on it."

I was surprised I could visibly tell Moses was old. He had gray hair around his black head, and old, tired-looking eyes. He looked gentle enough, but it could have been he was just worn-out.

The man yanked the old rusty tailgate down and Moses jumped out. There were no ewes in sight because, of course, they had fled to the other end of the pasture in response to the grand entry of a truck. Moses didn't look around for them either. He just lowered his head and started eating.

The man drove out the driveway, leaving all of us staring at the ram. We waited and waited. Nothing was happening. What a letdown.

I think we unconsciously imagined the ram would look at us straight in the eye and say, "Wow! What an awesome pasture you have prepared for me and my ewes. The ewes are knockouts! They look radiant. You must have flushed them. Thank you very, very much! I see cold running water and a feeding trough . . . Wow! This is definitely Sheep Heaven."

But we all went about our chores, hoping that nature would take its course.

About a week later I mentioned to Honey that I hadn't seen the ram "with" the ewes yet. "Honey, do you think Moses is too old?"

Two of our children yelled across the house, "He isn't too old!"

Good Grain

We are to use our time, talents, and treasures diligently to serve God completely in whatever we do. We must do our work out of love for God and those we serve, not for the reward.

Serve wholeheartedly, as if you were serving the Lord, not men, because you know that the Lord will reward everyone for whatever good he does, whether he is slave or free. (Ephesians 6:7–8)

I had very little knowledge about breeding that first summer. I didn't know who was bred and who wasn't. Honey ordered the SID *Sheepman's Production Handbook* for me the following year. For our second lambing season, I knew to mark the ram with colored chalk, and he would then imprint the ewe he bred so we could easily write down the ewes who would be expecting.

I also learned that there were many variables that affected the ewe's ability to conceive. The most surprising to me was how much light, temperature, and humidity control was needed to preserve a ewe's ability to conceive and to keep the embryo alive.

Breeding was primarily controlled by the light-to-dark ratio, meaning that as the days became shorter, more ewes would be able to conceive. That is why fertility is the highest and most efficient in September, October, and November, when the light exposure is only between ten and twelve hours.

I learned that the cooler the temperature, the greater the fertility and the better chance the embryo will survive. For example, if it is ninety degrees on the day of breeding, I could expect zero embryos to survive. Also, the humidity should be a constant 60 to 65 percent or lower throughout their breeding and pregnancy.

A low body temperature is also crucial for ewes. For example, body temperature rises in ewes that are required to walk long distances for their feed and water during warm weather. Also, if they eat too much in warm weather, their body temperature will rise. A fat ewe is more susceptible to heat stress than ewes in good condition.

I also found out that flushing the ewes will not advance the breeding season, but it will influence the ovulation rates early in the season and should produce an increased lambing rate! Yea for flushing!

I blindly believed all our ewes were expecting and began sharing at the dinner table everything I was learning about *dystocia*, which means "difficult births." I was getting a lot of "gross!" and "oh no!" comments. I soon had everyone a little antsy . . . I didn't want to be the only one! The whole family was now fully absorbed into my scary sheep project.

I made a copy of the most frequent birthing presentations from the trade publication *Best of Sheep!* and tacked them to the bulletin board in the barn so we'd have quick reference. Next to the diagrams the author had in big black letters, "Normal lambing is explosive, compared to cattle." Not the message I needed to read every day, but I knew we could handle whatever happened as long as we depended on the Master Shepherd. I was now praying daily for the ewes and us.

> I have strength for all things in Christ Who empowers me [I am ready for anything and equal to anything through Him Who infuses inner strength into me; I am self-sufficient in Christ's sufficiency]. (Philippians 4:13 AMP)

A pregnant ewe slowly enlarges with her lambs. She carries them for five months before delivery. She will normally birth her lambs within thirty to forty minutes after hard labor begins and the membranes rupture. On a breech or other difficult birth that prevents the water bag expulsion, she won't even go into labor. While watching the ewe and seeing no progress, we would then have to give her an exam, discern the lamb's position, and deliver accordingly. I was reading and praying the Scriptures on fear.

Fear not [there is nothing to fear], for I am with you; do not look around you in terror and be dismayed, for I am your God. I will strengthen and harden you to difficulties, yes, I will help you; yes, I will hold you up and retain you with My [victorious] right hand of rightness and justice. (Isaiah 41:10 AMP)

Every article I read on lambing sounded so matter-of-fact, so simple, so black-and-white. Do this, and that will happen. What situations come without attachments? There is always an unknown factor or two. Anxiety started whispering in my ear, "Are you prepared? Your advanced algebra test is in two weeks."

"But, sir, I'm only in the first grade."

"He said to me, My grace is sufficient for you, for my power is made perfect in weakness." Therefore I will boast all the more gladly about my weaknesses, so that Christ's power may rest on me. (2 Corinthians 12:9)

The Shearing Shed

Here I am again, Lord, on the barnyard floor. Shear away my mistrust in your power to work through a weak and fearful person like myself. I had pitied the sheep for not trusting in me; now where is my trust in you? I am both an ignorant sheep and a fearful shepherd. Forgive me, for I know that when your power is displayed in weak people, others are encouraged and you are glorified.

The surreal days of the summer past, with the ewes peacefully grazing on the rolling pasture, looking so beautiful, so English, demanding absolutely nothing from me, were pure bliss for a short period of time, but are now a fading memory.

chapter five

RED-HOT UDDERS

Walking into the barn was like walking into a Sub-Zero freezer. I feared that if the temperature dropped one degree lower, I'd have a flock of frozen stiffs! I called Milo and asked him if I should close up the barn and bring in some heat.

Milo assured me the ewes are healthier in an open barn that has fresh, cold air blowing through it. He informed me that a tight, humid barn can cause pneumonia.

"You don't want nu-moan-ya! No, sir! Keep the barn open. And don't you go worrying about the lambs; their mamas won't let them freeze. No, sir!"

I felt comforted by Milo's advice, and I trusted him. He was my neighbor.

I was getting fed up with having to get dressed in a nongender Ski Doo snowmobile suit every few hours and fight my way through blowing snowdrifts, just so I could arrive at an inhospitable, freezing barn. I was also sick of beating the frozen water buckets on the side of the barn and filling them again with ice water that evenly encased my huge snowmobile gloves. But worst of all was the acute disappointment I felt every time I opened the barn door and, there they were, my fat ewes, still pregnant! I was starting to believe they would be pregnant until the end of time.

The heavy, rounded ewes were doing the same thing and standing in the same spot as the day before, chewing their cud and staring into oblivion. Every day was the same, well, except for their udders. I suspected a little milkman was coming in every morning and pumping up those udders . . . trying to see how big they could get before they exploded.

The kids were all asleep. Honey made a roaring fire in the fireplace, and I made a huge batch of popcorn. We snuggled under our comforter, watched an old movie, and ate to our hearts' content, choosing to ignore the sheep world out there in the biting arctic.

Our wonderful evening was soon over, and it was time to make the dreaded evening barn check. I decided to skip it that night; *Just this once*, I told myself, disregarding the fact that tonight could be *the* night. I jumped in bed, feeling just a little guilty. I couldn't sleep. My mind was being attacked by an invasion of imaginary unthinkable horrors that could be happening at that very moment to our ewes' red-hot and stretched-to-the-limit udders!

I jumped up, slipped my cold snowmobile suit on over my pajamas, skipped the socks, and put the huge snowmobile boots on my bare feet and quickly made the agonizing, desolate trek to the barn. It was lightly snowing but blowing so hard I could hardly see the barn door.

Once I shut the heavy wooden barn door I could hear the monotonous chewing of cud. And there they were, fat as ever, chewing and staring into space like zombies.

I counted the ewes as usual and discovered one was missing. *Surely I miscounted.* Before I was able to recount, a ewe came charging in the small paddock door with ear-deafening bleats. It was Heidi, and she was in a panic. I watched with horror as she ran out the door again with her red-hot udder swinging precariously, and something didn't look right. I squeezed through the small doorway and looked into the paddock. The black night was so stuffed with blurring snow, I couldn't see her. I followed her cries and found her in the back right corner of the paddock, circling like a dog after its tail. When she saw me, she propelled back into the barn. I followed her in and finagled her into one of our newly built lambing pens and closed the gate behind us.

We were alone. She was breathing heavily, and her eyes were bulging out in terror. She swirled around, and then the terror struck me. Heidi's lamb was partially delivered and lifeless. The lamb's tongue was protruding out of its mouth. It was a ghastly gray color, and it looked frozen. In fact, the lamb was half-covered with snow. I couldn't believe what I was seeing; it was too nightmarish. I managed a quick "Help!" to the Lord.

I pushed Heidi in the corner of the pen with a super-strength that amazed me. I held her so hard she couldn't budge, and I checked her out. Only by the grace of God did I remember reading that sometimes a very large lamb will get stuck at the shoulders during delivery, and it was a fairly easy position to rectify. The article had a drawing of the problem delivery with a step-by-step diagram to remedy it. I had studied the diagram, and at the time, it didn't look like a big deal. It didn't look or feel anything like this frightening, heart-pounding, real-life scenario I was experiencing.

Without consciously thinking, I perfectly modeled the diagram. I tipped the head, pushed it back in until the shoulder was released, and then maneuvered the shoulder sideways as instructed.

I was totally unprepared to see Heidi quickly and easily deliver our first lamb. The lamb gently slipped onto the straw and instantly stood up, as big as life.

I yelled out, "It's a girl!" But there wasn't anyone to hear me. She stretched and just stood there, maybe dazed a little. *She's a real live lamb* . . . I wiped away my tears before they froze to my eyelashes.

Heidi began licking her lamb, and the lamb never moved an

inch. I thought it must feel like a good massage. Heidi cleaned her lamb until her wool was dry and curly. Then to my horror, she began to consume every sign of afterbirth that was in the stall. I was repulsed. I would later learn that her mission to eliminate the scent of blood was an innate genetic trait in birthing animals to keep their newborns concealed from predators. She was just doing her job.

I refused to let Heidi's excessive cleanup job ruin this beautiful miracle of birth for me. I didn't care that Heidi didn't have twins. I loved Heidi. I loved her very huge lamb. I loved the barn. I happily replaced her frozen-solid ice bucket with water. I climbed up the hayloft in my clumsy snowmobile boots and brought down our best hay for her as a reward. I cut open a new bale of fresh, golden straw and covered her stall. I didn't even know I was freezing. But I did know I would call our first lamb "Grace."

> Let us then approach the throne of grace with confidence, so that we may receive mercy and find grace to help us in our time of need. (Hebrews 4:16)

Honey stumbled through the barn door, half-awake. I knew he would be concerned when I didn't return right away. As soon as he saw the lamb, he grinned and disappeared. Within minutes he came back wheeling a huge, old scale on wheels that came with the barn.

"Step on the scale, and I'll get your weight."

"But, Honey, I'm wearing a heavy snowmobile suit and boots and my gloves must weigh a ton! And . . ."

"You're worrying about your weight? Tonight? Women!"

I can't believe I said that . . .

Honey shook his head, smiled, and weighed me. Then he weighed me holding the lamb. After doing a little math, he discovered Grace weighed an amazing fifteen pounds! The average weight of a newborn lamb is usually around seven pounds. The girls eventually called Grace "Big Gracie," and the name stuck.

~)

Lambing was completely new to us. We didn't know what to expect, what was normal, or when there was a real problem. We learned lambing that first winter by trial and many errors.

I read and reread every word in the trade publication *Best of Sheep!* In the article, "Tips for the Shepherd-Midwife," I was told to make sure the mothers' teats weren't plugged after giving birth and to stay in the pen until I saw her lambs nursing. They didn't tell me the mothers wouldn't like us milking their sore, hot udders. They didn't mention the lambs wouldn't be able to find their mothers' teats right away, and if they did find them, they were too weak to nurse, or she might not be ready for them to nurse. It didn't say most of the lambs would act brain-dead for a while! We watched with horror as they tried to nurse their water buckets, their twins, or our pant legs. We were a wreck. We tried so hard to get the lambs nursing that we exasperated the lambs, their mothers, and ourselves.

Eventually we recognized that what was going on was normal and that we should leave them all alone for a while. Left in peace, the moms would patiently nudge their babies to them until they finally drank the life-giving colostrum. And we did learn to recognize when a lamb or a mother was really in trouble, and how to help them.

I remember wanting to write a manual for other apprentice shepherds. Today, I would call the book *Lambing for Dummies*.

It was exciting to see the birth of so many twins and triplets. They were too precious for words. And the sheep man was right; they were all different colors and patterns. I loved the polka-dotted lambs the best. Thankfully Heidi was the only ewe that delivered a single lamb. The kids pleaded her case by reminding me Grace weighed as much as twins. We never culled Heidi. The following year she was bred to a registered Columbia ram and delivered beautiful, pure white, eight-pound twins.

It was very interesting to see how differently each mother handled her newborns. Some were overly fastidious in their nurturing, while others seemed very blasé about the whole "mother" thing and kept losing their babies. Both extremes caused the lambs and us some problems. The well-balanced mothers needed very little help from us, and their lambs thrived and made us look good.

I got to the point where I couldn't wait to enter the barn, and I had a hard time leaving it. It was now a distinct, special new world full of life and sweet, clean smells. I started calling this world "Sheep World." I discovered that time moved very slowly in Sheep World; slow enough to appreciate everything that was going on. No matter how hard I was working, I always felt rested when I left. Even after mucking out a stall!

I especially loved the beautiful music reverberating throughout Sheep World during the lambing season. The notes were made by the sweet interchange between the moms and their babies, with soft little baas and the lyrical munching of hay. I was totally enthralled by this unique symphony and the spectacular dramas taking place in each sheep pen.

One night I asked the Lord to help me remember exactly what I was seeing and hearing in the barn, because I wanted to be forever thankful to him. That night I realized that my raising sheep was really his idea. Eventually we would see hundreds of people blessed by his gift, but that night, it was his gift to me.

Offer hospitality to one another without grumbling. Each one should use whatever gift he has received to serve others, faithfully administering God's grace in its various forms. (1 Peter 4:9–10)

chapter six

SNIP, DIP, AND CLIP

The notes I took from *Countryside* magazine, in "The Sheep Shed" section read, "snip, dip, and clip the lambs at birth." After a few embarrassing phone calls to Milo after Big Gracie was born, I wrote down the obvious meaning: Snip the umbilical cord at birth, dip it in 7 percent iodine, and clip the tail off at three days old. *Now, why didn't they just say that?* We did the snipping and the dipping okay, and now it was time to do the clipping.

I had no idea lambs had to have their tails cut off. I surprised myself the day I found out . . . I didn't get all unglued and unhinged! I had been depending on the Lord for one scary task after another, and I finally realized God would be with me and enable me. I didn't feel alone anymore . . . I had a helper.

> So we say with confidence, "The Lord is my helper; I will not be afraid." (Hebrews 13:6)

"Well, Lord, I have another ghastly, hideous, and mind-boggling assignment. I have to cut the tails off my precious lambs. But it's okay. I know you'll be with me."

He who trusts in himself is a fool, but he who walks in wisdom is kept safe (Proverbs 28:26).

In other words, A wise person depends on God!

Honey came home from work and shocked me by announcing he would take care of clipping the tails. I couldn't believe it! I was all ready to watch the Lord help me with this beastly assignment, and now I didn't have to.

"You mean I really don't have to do it? You are going to do it? With a knife?"

"I said I'll take care of it!"

I couldn't believe it. Honey couldn't even watch the fake operations on TV. Then I heard him on the phone. A few minutes later he announced to the whole family that a neighbor shepherd was coming over after dinner to cut the tails. *I should have known!* He yelled out with all the commanding force of his authority, "Listen up, everyone, next lambing season *we* are going to cut the tails, so watch closely!"

The family march to the barn was silent except for the crunching of snow beneath our feet. The night seemed darker than usual, but it was okay; it agreed with our hearts.

"Now we can see a real shepherd at work."

Everyone gave me a nasty look, just for breaking the silence. No one wanted to hear any small talk. The neighbor shepherd arrived at our barn before we did. He greeted all of us with a cheery, but perhaps questioning look. We must have looked rather funereal. He acted as though nothing unusual was going to take place in our barn that night, and for some reason that comforted me.

Honey asked him, "What can I get you? Do you need anything?"

"I'll need a good light and some blood-stopping powder."

Honey scurried around and plugged in a heat lamp where

he was standing but told him we didn't have any blood-stopping powder.

"I kind of figured that, so I brought some I had. But you'll need a bucket."

"What is the bucket for?" I innocently asked.

"For the tails."

"Oh."

The neighbor shepherd skillfully cut off our precious little newborns' tails with his knife, and then he sprinkled their stubs with the bright blue blood-stopping powder he brought with him. When I put the lambs back with their mothers, they wagged their little stubs, as they always do when they approach their moms, and blood sprinkled everywhere. Our innocent little lambs were now desecrated and obviously in pain. They were hunched over, and they walked very, very deliberately.

I think the neighbor was trying to put a smile on our sour faces as he said cheerfully, "Looks like your lambs are patriotic. They're all red, white, and blue."

Unlike our normal gracious response to people, every one of us jerked our heads, looked this man straight in the eye, and delivered the meanest, most despicable, nasty look we could muster.

I couldn't get to sleep that night. I knew we were wrong to treat our neighbor the way we did. He came to help. I was very sorry and decided to bring him a loaf of pumpkin bread I had baked that morning. But I still couldn't get to sleep. I kept hearing the *thud, thud, thud* in the bucket. And over and over I relived the upsetting moment when our family realized the bucket was full to the top with tails still warm.

Then one of the kids asked, "Mom, what do we do with this bucket of tails?"

I asked Honey, "What do we do with a bucket of lambs' tails?"

Honey never answered me. He just took the bucket . . . somewhere.

We never got used to cutting the tails, but we knew if we didn't do it, the lambs would be plagued with pests and infections. With enablement from the Lord, we did what had to be done.

> Those who trust in the Lord are like Mount Zion, which cannot be shaken but endures forever. (Psalm 125:1)

About a month after lambing season, a package came in the mail, and it was addressed to me. Honey had ordered a top-of-the-line electric docker. This tool could cut a lamb's tail and sear the wound in one operation. I couldn't think of any gift in the whole world I would rather have had that day . . . even though it looked like a medieval torturer's scariest instrument of horror!

Our family would have been so consoled the night our lambs' tails were cut if they could have seen the future. The following year, Honey plugged in the new docker, and I held the lambs. I had to hold them really tight because they would convulse for a second while letting out a loud, "Baaaaaaa!" Then they passed out in my arms. But by the time I walked them back to their moms, they would be totally alert, in no pain, and happily wagging their dry little stumps.

Good Grain

The Good Shepherd is able to use our circumstances, no matter how painful, for our long-range good. But this promise can only be claimed by those who know and love the Shepherd and trust in him . . . not in themselves or in Sheep World.

And we know that in all things God works for the good of those who love him, who have been called according to his purposes. (Romans 8:28)

Chew on This

We all have experienced or will experience the Shepherd's knife. We may even experience a piercing, passing-out level of loss. But remember, we're in his arms, and he's holding us tight against his heart. Sometimes the Shepherd will wield the knife to cut out a part of our lives that harbors the plaguing pests. Sometimes we feel the knife just because we live in a fallen world of war, disease, accidents, and hurting people.

Like the sheep, we may never understand why our Shepherd allows our knifelike disappointments and tragedies. We must remember that he is God and we are not. We are his sheep, and he is our Shepherd . . . sent to us by our Creator. He is asking us to put all our trust in him. His picture is bigger than our picture.

A BUMMER LAMB

"Come quick; it's Susan! She just had triplets!"

"Mom, hurry! Something is wrong!"

Sure enough, Susan was butting one of her lambs away. She was accepting two of her lambs and rejecting the third one.

We didn't know that day that once a ewe rejects a lamb, she will never change her mind. Not grasping the full measure of persistence in a stubborn sheep, we tried for several disheartening and frustrating hours to get her to accept her bewildered lamb.

"You hold the mother, and I'll put the lamb up to her."

"The lamb won't nurse! Let me try squirting the milk in his mouth."

"He won't drink it."

"He's hurting! Let me hold him for a few minutes, and we'll try again."

Finally, when absolutely nothing worked and the lamb was looking worse, we realized the ewe's decision was set in cement, and we should probably quit. We didn't like Susan anymore, and we were outraged and temporarily disillusioned with sheep again. We were all torn up watching this mother sheep physically and emotionally abusing her baby.

He was a little boy lamb, snow white with big, black eyes and the saddest face you ever saw. Every time this little guy approached his mom, she would butt him away. The more persistent he was, the more power she would put in her butts, until finally, he was hitting the wall of the pen. The girls were crying.

"Mother, do something! Call Dad!"

Dad walked into the barn, took one look at what was going on, and said, "This little guy really looks bad. You had better do something!"

I didn't know what to do. I had never heard of a ewe rejecting her own lamb. I didn't know it was so common that the sheep industry called these lambs "bummer lambs."

"Let's try one more time," someone said for the umpteenth time.

We forcefully held the mother against the wall of the pen so she couldn't butt him; but as we brought the lamb up to her teat to nurse, the angry ewe stamped her feet again with such force, I thought her legs would splinter. We got the message. By now the little guy was all hunched over. His head was hanging so low I thought there might be something wrong with his neck, but it was his spirit. We didn't realize this little guy had been getting wounded every time his mom gave him the thumbs-down refusal, and he was now "rejection personified." Then he started shivering, and when he clamped his dry mouth shut and wouldn't even lick the milk I was squirting at him, I knew he had given up.

"I'm bringing him into the house now. We'll give him a houseful of mothers and a dad to boot."

Everyone clapped and hooted, and our youngest daughter yelled out between sobs, "We'll take you to our house, and you'll be ours forever and ever!"

The forever and ever didn't sound right to me, but I would take things one step at a time. I just knew that today, this lamb belonged with us.

I reached down and brought the limp, starving little lamb up to my neck, softly pressing my cheek against his tiny, bony head and walked carefully to the house. In the holding of him, I thought he might be a breakable porcelain treasure.

He reached down from on high and took hold of me; he drew me out of deep waters. (Psalm 18:16)

Honey ran in the house smiling and proudly announced, "Here you go, straight from your local grain elevator . . . a twenty-five-pound bag of Merrick's Super Lamb Milk Replacer, filled with vitamins and minerals, with the instructions on the back. Now I'm off to work, again. Good luck with the lamb."

Honey loved to find solutions to our problems . . . what a guy!

I would later learn there is no artificial substitute for the mother's first milk, colostrum. In other words, you can't buy it. Our little guy didn't get his mother's first milk, and the death rate for lambs without it is 50 percent. The ewes' antibodies are not transferred to their young while in the uterus, so the lambs have to drink it as newborns to get this protection. Death most often comes from septicemia, pneumonia, or arthritis.

An ingenious tip I read about later would tell me to milk several of our ewes as soon as their colostrum came in, put it in ice cube trays, and freeze it for future orphans. Our first orphan lamb did not have this protection, but he did have our love.

I carefully force-fed our delicate treasure a smidgen of his powdered milk, and he opened his eyes. The kids were oohing and ahhing. A little later, when he started sucking the bottle himself, everyone clapped, and when he burped, everyone snickered. He had a noisy support group.

I explained to the kids how painful and fatal rejection can be and that I still wasn't sure if this little guy would make it. But I did know he wouldn't have a chance unless we lavished him with huge doses of love. With tear-streaked faces, the kids responded, "We'll give it to him, Mom!"

"Let me take him first."

"No, I will. I'm the oldest."

"I'll give him his next bottle, and he can have my blue quilt."

"I'll write up the feeding schedule and put it on the kitchen desk."

"Mom, when he's done eating, can I rock him?"

"Can I rock him after she does?"

But those who suffer he delivers in their suffering;
> he speaks to them in their affliction.

He is wooing you from the jaws of distress
> to a spacious place free from restriction
> to the comfort of your table laden with choice food.

(Job 36:15–16)

Good Grain

Because of the great servant love of his shepherd, our orphaned lamb really was born again. While he was near death and in a totally hopeless state, unconditional love came to him. It was a love he didn't deserve; after all, he was only a sheep. In the midst of great pain and rejection, his master came and filled him with warm, soothing milk . . . milk he didn't have the strength to drink himself. Hopelessness and despair had looked to win, but instead, hope poured in with all its glory. Now, in the arms of his shepherd, he could rest. He would be taken care of completely, forever.

chapter eight

THE ADOPTION

"Uh-oh. I think we need diapers!"

I made a trip into town and bought a box of boys' preemie diapers with blue trim. I hoped I didn't run into anyone at the store, because I knew what I was doing sounded kind of kooky; you know, a little off kilter. But just a little.

We named our little guy Joey. Everyone carried him around like a baby. The kids rocked him and sang to him, and when we weren't fussing with him, our German shepherd was. She would lie next to him and gently lick him all over, just like his mother should have done. She also perceived him as a delicate treasure.

After about two days we could see Joey's little arched back getting lower, his head becoming more erect, and his eyes appearing brighter. Joey was choosing to live. We would later discover that not all rescued lambs choose life.

> I have set before you life and death, blessings and curses. Now choose life, so that you and your children may live and that you may love the LORD your God, listen to his voice, and hold fast to him. (Deuteronomy 30:19b–20a)

Our daughters grained and watered their horses every morning before school. In fact, they were often known to feed, groom, and ride before the school bus arrived. Horses were their passion. During the lambing season, our daughters graciously gave the ewes their morning grain and made the "lamb check" as well. They would look for newborns that had the telltale sign of rejection . . . a hunched back and a drooping head. They removed these lambs immediately from their abusive mothers and brought them into the house for the "love treatment" before it was too late.

> From birth I was cast upon you; from my mother's womb you have been my God. (Psalm 22:10)

> Although my father and my mother have forsaken me, yet the Lord will take me up (and adopt me as his child). (Psalm 27:10 TLB)

I visited several large sheep farms to see how the pros handled their "bummer lambs." They told me there were all kinds of situations that caused newborns to be orphaned. Some mothers died at birth; some had mastitis, a painful infection in their udders. Others would only accept two lambs and reject their third or fourth lamb. (They must have known they only had two teats and would have the hard duty of teaching their youngsters how to share!) One shepherd told me that every so often he'd see a new mother so frightened and agitated after giving birth that she wanted nothing to do with her babies. She just wanted to flee.

Often, he said, it's the lamb's fault. Some newborns are too weak to nurse, or they become injured or crippled during birth. And in a large operation, they will often get separated from their mothers after birth. I now realized every orphaned lamb has his or her own unique but tragic story.

This shepherd took me to where he kept his orphans. I was shocked to see multiple stalls filled with skinny little newborns with rounded tummies, sucking away on nipples sticking out the sides of buckets. They seemed to be content with their pseudomothers. Other orphans were nursing from lactating goats that were locked in stanchions, and they also seemed okay. I asked the shepherd, "How come these rejected lambs are doing so well?"

"Because I got them out of the rejecting ewe's stall right away. An abused lamb will lose his desire to live."

Every shepherd I visited confessed to giving their badly abused or injured lambs personal care for a period of two to three days . . . usually in their home. Now they were talking my language.

We continued to bring every orphaned lamb into our home for a minimum of three days. It gave them an awesome start, and besides, we weren't dealing with hundreds of lambs, so we could do it. And who's kidding who? We loved it!

Before we knew it, the spirit of rejection in Joey was completely gone, and we had a brand-new, born-again, thriving lamb, bouncing and leaping around our house. It didn't take him long to figure out who was who in the family either.

If the girls weren't around, Joey came to me for his bottle. You know, me, the now quickly aging mother who is married to "Honey." Just like Mary's lamb, Joey followed me wherever I went.

Joey never imposed himself on Honey . . . and when Honey did pick him up, he sat so still and proper. Maybe it was Honey's deep, commanding voice that made Joey sense he was the "big guy." I like to imagine he had respect for the father, the family's protector and provider, the one who literally created Sheep World and our home.

Joey joined up with our son Jimmy for fun. Our family will never forget watching and hearing the two of them run around the house at high speed. They would slip and slide around the kitchen island, run up and down the stairs, and inevitably Joey would skip the last four steps and glide through the air. What a sight! Of course, they would keep it up until someone would yell, "That's enough, you two! Quiet! We're trying to study!"

Joey was one of the kids. One of the Father's kids.

As he says in Hosea: "I will call them 'my people' who are not my people; and I will call her 'my loved one' who is not my loved one," and, "It will happen that in the very place where it was said to them, 'You are not my people,' they will be called 'sons of the living God.'" (Romans 9:25–26)

~

If you are wondering who is who in our family, I'd love to give you a quick peek at our six children the year Joey invaded their spaces.

Jerry is our firstborn. He seriously collected bugs and plants as a little guy, loved hiking, and dreamed of living off the land. It was no surprise when Jerry wanted to major in biology at college. It was very painful for Jerry and for us to see him leave just as we moved into the farm! Jerry and Ann Vaughn married and have two children. Jerry is a scientist in Research & Development at LABS, Inc., in Denver. We coveted his visits home! It was during his first spring break he met our adopted lamb, Joey.

The year Joey was born, our oldest daughter, Lynn, was a senior in high school. She was our blonde-haired, athletic, caring, and responsible young woman. Lynn enjoyed her beautiful buckskin mare, Lady, and our newly acquired sheep until college rightly took over her life. Lynn achieved her goal of becoming a registered nurse. She married Bill Young and chose to work part time (evenings) so she could be a stay-at-home mom with their four children.

Jill was our outgoing, black-haired freshman in high school who excelled in academics, communication, and track. Jill enjoyed fast rides and long excursions around the property on her horse, Pistol, who was a trained English Jumper. Jill and her sisters often rode their horses into our thirty-foot-deep pond to swim . . . while I prayed. Jill majored in Chemistry in college and worked for Dow Chemical Company. She married Steve Sklenar, and she chose to be a stay-at-home-mom to raise their four children.

I called our brown-haired seventh grader, Jane, my "assistant shepherd." Jane eventually trained five horses, and with her sisters, she competed at numerous horse shows; their bedrooms were full of ribbons. Jane also excelled in track, and she became a high school track coach and taught children with learning disabilities. Jane married David Marthaler and is a busy stay-at-home mom raising four children.

The year we adopted Joey, our youngest daughter, Anne, was a little, black-eyed third grader who amazingly kept up with her sisters and brother. She even joined them at the local college for a six-week class on horse care, which hit the local newspaper. Anne was fearless. In the third grade Ann was riding a small Shetland pony, and before high school, she was training and showing her fiery palomino. She also excelled in track and academics and received her bachelor of education degree. Anne married Sam Ulstad and is a proud stay-at-home mom of five children.

Jimmy was and precocious preschooler the year Joey was born. By age five, he was riding Anne's pony at top speed, but would have preferred a motorbike. He graduated from the University of Michigan, receiving a letter from the Varsity Track team. Jim married Shannon Koss and they have two children. He is now a partner of a wealth management firm. Jimmy was and continues to be a gifted communicator who loves people. He has his own set of hilarious sheep stories (that probably shouldn't be told) and has had audiences roaring.

I didn't want to call the neighbor over to cut Joey's tail, but I did. I reluctantly headed for the barn with a humongous lump in my throat and with Joey following close behind me. My poor little lamb . . . so innocent. It was obvious he was ecstatic to be on an excursion to the barn, as he was bouncing and running circles around me. I quickly handed him over to the neighbor while reminding myself, "The knife is for his good." (This was before the electric docker came into our lives.)

The cut was very painful for him, and like all the other lambs, he was covered with blue blood-stopping powder and sprinkles of fresh blood. He looked like a bad accident.

I discovered Joey still trusted me, even though I had his tail cut off. When I gave him his baby shots, he didn't give me any resistance, but his little heart was pounding so hard. I hurt. It would be easy to raise sheep if they were all my adopted kids!

I'll never forget opening the door to the laundry room in the morning to let Joey out. He would literally jump for joy when he saw me. He would be so ecstatic he'd start bouncing like a basketball and wouldn't stop until I grabbed him in midair and held him close for a few seconds. I loved that kid. He discovered that he would not be alone in the dark forever . . . I would always open the door in the morning.

> Answer me quickly, O LORD; my spirit fails. Do not hide your face from me or I will be like those who go down to the pit. Let the morning bring me word of your unfailing love, for I have put my trust in you. (Psalm 143:7–8)

The Shearing Shed

Lord, when I feel like I'm locked in a dark room for what seems like forever, remind me that eventually morning will come . . . a new day will arrive. Replace my fear, doubt, and unbelief with faith, hope, and trust in you!

chapter nine

HEAVEN HAS BLUE CARPET

And God raised us up with Christ and seated us with him in the
heavenly realms in Christ Jesus, in order that in the coming ages
he might show the incomparable riches of his grace, expressed in
his kindness to us in Christ Jesus. (Ephesians 2:6–7)

Joey was brought into our home and experienced things that were
unbelievable to the other residents of Sheep World. No barn straw
for Joey—he was living on the soft, luxurious blue carpet that was
throughout his master's house.

Joey was rocked to sleep, watched cartoons with Ann and Jimmy,
rode in the car with Lynn, was covered with kisses, wrapped in flan-
nel blankets, and became the center of attention with every visitor.

"He's sooo cute! He's darrrling! Can I hold him?"

Little Joey just snuggled up in everyone's neck and would have
purred (if lambs could).

No eye has seen,
no ear has heard,
no mind has conceived
what God has prepared for those who love him. (1 Corinthians 2:9)

Joey would have been called a bummer lamb by the sheep
industry because most shepherds considered these orphans a nui-
sance. I now believe the bummers are the winners. Who in all of

Sheep World experienced a taste of heaven? Our little bummer, Joey. Who took naps on soft carpet? Joey. Who was personally cared for by the shepherd and his family? Joey. Because Joey *chose* to live and *allowed* us to love him, he became the most blessed lamb in our entire flock!

> Immense in mercy and with an incredible love, he embraced us. He took our sin-dead lives and made us alive in Christ. He did all this on his own, with no help from us! Then he picked us up and set us down in highest heaven in company with Jesus, our Messiah. Now God has us where he wants us, with all the time in this world and the next to shower grace and kindness upon us in Christ Jesus. Saving is all his idea, and all his work. All we do is trust him enough to let him do it. It's God's gift from start to finish! (Ephesians 2:5–8 MSG)

The apostle Paul was taken up into paradise and heard "inexpressible things, things that man is not permitted to tell" (2 Corinthians 12:4). He didn't know if he was taken up in his body or in his spirit, but he did know he was in paradise (the third heaven). This spiritual experience has happened to a wide variety of people from all walks of life since the resurrection of Jesus Christ. Today we are able to hear their experiences through our various forms of media. The message that there really is a *paradise*, an unbelievable *heaven* is finally getting out to the whole world, one personal story at a time.

> "I know a man in Christ who fourteen years ago was caught up to the third heaven. Whether it was in the body or out of the body I do not know—God knows. And I know that this man—whether in the body or apart from the body I do not know, but God knows—was caught up to paradise. He heard inexpressible things, things that man is not permitted to tell." (2 Corinthians 12: 2–4)

Good Grain

If life has made you feel like a bummer, take heart. God intends for you to be a winner and the blessed one. First, always *choose* life and *allow* the Good Shepherd to embrace and care for you. Then be prepared—he just might pick you up and set you down in the highest heaven.

P.S. Let me know if you're standing on blue carpet.

A word of warning came from Honey, "You better not keep Joey here too long or he'll expect blue carpet for the rest of his life!"

The Shearing Shed

We all have to grow up. Not just physically and mentally, but spiritually . . . and it isn't all roses! The new life we receive from our Savior is just the beginning. Our Shepherd will put each one of us on a unique path that will enable us to mature as his people and eventually walk out our destiny. We will go through many tests in faith, hope, and love at various levels. If we don't pass, we'll be taking the same test over and over until we do.

Hint: Whatever you do, don't resist, complain, or grumble about the path the Shepherd has put you on or you might end up walking in circles for forty years, like the grumbling Israelites.

I knew he was right, but it seemed too quick to let him go. I was just getting my new routine down pat and starting to enjoy my little companion. Joey never ventured more than a foot away from my feet. I remember being fascinated by the sound of his hooves clicking across the tile or down the driveway. And when he nestled up in my lap or curled into my neck, I was the one who purred (if people could).

> Just one day after Korah and his followers were executed for grumbling and complaining against God, the Israelites started all over with more muttering and complaining. Their negative attitude only caused them to rebel even more and to bring about even greater trouble. It eroded their faith in God and encouraged thoughts of giving up and turning back. The path to open rebellion against God begins with dissatisfaction and skepticism, then moves to grumbling about both God and present circumstances. Next come bitterness and resentment, followed finally by rebellion and open hostility . . . Beware! These attitudes lead to rebellion and separation from God.
> (Commentary on Numbers 16:41 from the *NIV Life Application Study Bible*)

Joey loved his bottle, but now he was inhaling it in about five seconds, and I realized he needed more than milk; he needed solid food and hay. Newborn lambs watch their moms munch on hay as soon as they are born. They start imitating them by mouthing a strand or two. After weeks of mouthing the hay, they slowly start to chew it. Joey had never seen hay. Honey was right. It was time.

Our family had given this lamb a new life through our love and presence, but now we would have to take him back into Sheep World where he could mature and reach his purpose and destiny.

Chew on This

A spiritually mature person has centered his or her whole life on Jesus and his Words of Life. It means that there is nothing or no one more important to them than Christ. Some very young people are spiritually mature, while some very old people are still drinking milk from the Shepherd's bottle!

But for right now, friends, I'm completely frustrated by your unspiritual dealings with each other and with God. You're acting like infants in relation to Christ, capable of nothing much more than nursing at the breast. Well, then, I'll nurse you since you don't seem capable of anything more. As long as you grab for what makes you feel good or makes you look important, are you really much different than a babe at the breast, content only when everything's going your way? (1 Corinthians 3:1 – 3 MSG)

chapter ten

NOT OF THIS WORLD

Joey was not prepared for the feel, the smells, the sounds, or the residents on his first visit to Sheep World.

I gently put him down on the straw and I whispered to him, "It's going to be okay, little guy; everything's going to be okay." I think I was reassuring myself. Joey walked around on the straw as if his little hooves were covered with glue. "What is this prickly stuff?" he seemed to say. He was used to walking on carpet.

Suddenly our two geese entered the barn, squawking. Their wings were flapping so hard you'd think they were on a runway, ready for liftoff, and they were honking so loud I was sure it could pierce the eardrums of the earless. I wasn't surprised that they skidded in to check out the new kid, because our self-appointed watchmen never missed a birth, a death, or a visitor on "their" farm. I grabbed Joey and held him close to me. I could feel his fear.

The horses started whinnying for me to get them out of their stalls. I held Joey tight in my left arm and quickly slid five stall doors open. We watched as the colossal quarter horses hightailed it down the middle walkway, spitting sawdust in every direction, going through the door into the daylight. It then appeared they hit an invisible wall. Burying their hind feet deep in the earth, they stopped dead in their tracks. Why? They decided to take a sand bath before hitting the buggy pasture. Very carefully they collapsed their legs, set their huge bodies down in the cool sand, and rolled over and over until they were completely covered. They jumped up, violently shaking off the excess, and after letting out monstrous amounts of disgusting gas, they ran out of sight into their very own kingdom. Unbridled, these well-trained animals appeared wild and beautiful. They wouldn't be seen near the barn until they were ready for a long, cool drink.

I noticed the geese had now joined the ewes in the high pasture. I shook my head and probably rolled my eyes because the geese were back to extracting bits and pieces of hay and grass out of the ewes' wool. This fetish of theirs seemed bizarre to me, but the fact that the ewes enjoyed it was even more freakish, because they never allowed anyone to touch them. Could it be these ewes, like most female species, were enjoying the attention their hairdressers were giving them?

It was finally quiet in the barn, and I set Joey back down on the straw. He was gently touching the hay with the tip of his nose when our two batches of multicolored kittens appeared on the scene, their mouths still wet from nursing. They scurried on top of the sheep stalls and then headed up to the high, wooden beams overhead. It was obvious they were showing off their newly acquired skills for us. Offensive squeals from our two piglets speared the silence and spooked the kittens—they scattered and disappeared in a flash. I picked up Joey before he, too, could find a hiding place and brought him back to the house for one more stress-free day on blue carpet.

Eventually Joey became indifferent to the noises and antics of his barn neighbors and started to enjoy the little guys that were just like him. One day I saw him run toward the stair ramp that takes the sheep outside into their paddock. He didn't walk down the ramp, but instead he took off like Superboy and glided over the stairs, landing on the ground. His landing was a little shaky, and I laughed as I thought, *This is Jimmy's influence!* A little later I saw him heading for the same ramp, only this time he had four lambs following him.

All five of them soared through the air, high over the stairs, and successfully landed in the paddock. They did it over and over until the crabby ewes broke it up. Joey was just doing what he had learned in the master's house.

> We do not want you to become lazy, but to imitate those who through faith and patience inherit what has been promised. (Hebrews 6:12)

At first Joey would be waiting at the gate when it was time for his bottle; his little tummy was his timepiece. He would be standing there all alone, looking worried, if that is possible, and relieved when I came. One day he stayed out in the pasture with the other lambs until I came. Of course, when he saw me coming, he ran so fast toward the gate that I was afraid he wouldn't be able to stop. But he did. I could see that Joey had lost his anxiety about my coming at feeding time. He now knew I would always come.

> So do not worry, saying, "What shall we eat?" or "What shall we drink?" or "What shall we wear?" For the pagans run after all these things, and your heavenly Father knows that you need them. But seek first his kingdom and his righteousness, and all these things will be given to you as well. (Matthew 6:31–33)

> I give waters in the wilderness and rivers in the desert, to give drink to My people, My chosen, the people I formed for Myself, that they may set forth My praise [and they shall do it]. (Isaiah 43:20b–21 AMP)

Living in Sheep World wasn't all gliding and flying for Joey. As much as he enjoyed his new friends, he found out their mothers were out to get him. He could only join up with the lambs when they strayed from their moms.

A nursing ewe will only nurse her own lamb, and any lamb who even thinks about getting close to her will get a hoof in the face. I saw Joey take a couple of really bad hits; both times he landed on the ground with such force I was afraid he was injured. Joey didn't have a mom to call to him and bleat, "It's okay, come to mama; have a sip of milk."

Chew on This

James 1:27 tells us that our Father in heaven counts religion as pure and faultless *if* we are looking after orphans and widows in their distress, and keeping ourselves from being polluted by the world. This would include the growing number of single moms with young children.

The U.S. Census Bureau estimates that on Mother's Day, May 8, 2005, there were 10 million single moms with children under the age of eighteen in our nation. This figure is up from 3 million in 1970.

Am I looking after the widows, orphans, or single moms with kids who live in my sphere of influence? Or am I so polluted with the things the world offers I don't even see them?

Quoting from *The Shepherd* magazine, "Orphan lambs or lambs in search of their mothers are butted by bully ewes. Broken ribs and necks along with dislocated necks frequently occur."

Joey was an orphan from Sheep World, where there are no adoptions, foster parents, grandmas, grandpas, aunts, or babysitters. An orphan stays an orphan in Sheep World.

Joey was alone and unwanted out there in Sheep World. So,

everyone in the family volunteered to make extra barn checks on him. Our first orphan lamb was experiencing rejection and physical abuse again, and we didn't know how he would handle it. We didn't know who was suffering the most, Joey or us.

> I have given them your word and the world has hated them, for they are not of the world any more than I am of the world. My prayer is not that you take them out of the world but that you protect them from the evil one. (John 17:14–15)

Joey continued to experience persecution from the ewes, but he never cowered or became depressed. Every once in a while he would mistakenly follow one of the lambs right to their mother's undersides, and the mother would proceed to deliver rapid kicks to his head. Joey always picked himself up from the ground and went on grazing, continuing to grow and thrive. He was really a remarkable and inspiring lamb.

As time went on, it was obvious that security was written all over Joey. He emanated an inner confidence that enabled him to walk fearlessly among the defensive ewes. He walked through their ranks oblivious to the butts and angry baas and was unaffected by their brutality. He carried himself with a regal demeanor never seen before in Sheep World. He appeared to be alone, but he wasn't. Our love was always in him. Joey didn't have a sheep father, mother, brother, or sister, but he knew he had more. The owner and master of all the sheep in Sheep World adopted him!

> But we also rejoice in our sufferings, because we know that suffering produces perseverance; perseverance, character; and character, hope. And hope does not disappoint us, because God has poured out his love into our hearts by the Holy Spirit, whom he has given us. (Romans 5:3–5)

Chew on This

Paul teaches that Christians are to live in such a radical way that people will know they are Christians. They are to be lights in a world that is getting darker every day. They are called to delight in weaknesses, insults, hardships, persecution, and difficulties. They are to bless those who persecute them; bless, not curse! They are never to repay anyone evil for evil. And if it is possible, they are to be at peace with everyone they know. Christians are not to be overcome by evil, but are called to overcome evil with good! (*Read Romans 12:9–21*)

Good Grain

Have you been kicked, butted, or rejected? Has your spirit been beaten down by sheep's hooves? Ask the Shepherd to lead you safely through the crowd of butters and bruisers to take refuge in him. Jesus heals the brokenhearted and binds up their wounds. His love always protects, always trusts, always hopes, and always perseveres. He delights in those who put their hope in his unfailing love!

(*Read Psalm 147 and 1 Corinthians 13:7.*)

When Joey would see me coming, he would leap in the air, straight up from a standing position. I'm sure there are little springs hidden in the feet of lambs. His reaction always delighted me. I wondered if all the distractions in the barn would eventually cause him to lose his single-minded devotion to me. Would he be a sheep that trusted in me or in the barn's treasures? Would the other sheep see him following me and do likewise? I would just have to wait and see.

> And now I'm afraid that exactly as the Snake seduced Eve with his smooth patter, you are being lured away from the simple purity of your love for Christ. (2 Corinthians 11:3 MSG)

> You have persevered and have endured hardship for my name, and have not grown weary. Yet I hold this against you: You have forsaken your first love. Remember the height from which you have fallen! Repent and do the things you did at first. If you do not repent, I will come to you and remove your lampstand from its place." (Revelation 2: 3–5 NIV)

We were all relieved to see Joey finally interacting with the other lambs on a regular basis. It began when we started the lambs on grain. Honey built a creep feeder with an entrance too narrow for the ewes to get in. The lambs would congregate around their very own feeder, totally indifferent to the wailing of their worried mothers. Of course, Joey was always right in the middle of the group. We called them "the Creep-Feed Gang."

I observed that when the lambs were separated from their mothers and standing around the creep feeder, they took on a new stance. They appeared a bit aloof, bored, and maybe cool—like teenagers. I was shocked to see this false sense of independence in the lambs. After getting their fill of grain, they returned to their mothers and behaved like little kids again.

Now that Joey was on grain, I was able to wean him from the bottle. He wasn't my baby anymore; he was grown-up and living his whole life in Sheep World now. He continued to stand out from the other sheep as an out-of-the-ordinary, rare, set-apart young ram. Why was he different? What set him apart? Instead of spending his whole life seeking after food, as the rest of the flock did, he was spending it seeking after me, his food-giver, his shepherd.

> Just as the living Father sent me and I live because of the Father, so the one who feeds on me will live because of me. This is the bread that came down from heaven. Your forefathers ate manna and died, but he who feeds on this bread will live forever. (John 6:56–58)

> I'm asking God for one thing, only one thing:
> To live with him in his house my whole life long.
> I'll contemplate his beauty; I'll study at his feet . . .
> My father and mother walked out and left me,
> But God took me in.
> (Psalm 27:4, MSG)

chapter eleven

THE SHEEP
OF MY PASTURE

"The miracles I do in my Father's name speak for me, but you do not believe because you are not my sheep. My sheep listen to my voice; I know them, and they follow me." (John 10:25b–27)

Joey responded with enthusiasm whenever I entered the barn or the pasture. I loved his radical response. He was the only sheep on the farm that knew me; all the others totally ignored my presence. They were so content in their self-centered and inclusive little lives that they couldn't see or hear me. They were all about "me, myself, and what's mine." They would go into war mode when anyone, man or sheep, tried to intrude upon the boundaries they had so rigidly set up around themselves.

My orphan lamb had experienced rescue, adoption, hugs, and discipline from my hands, plus grand rides to town in our Suburban and adventures to unknown pastures on our hay wagon. But the sheep that refused to follow me had no idea that there was more to life than their little world. Their ignorance caused them to live isolated and rigid lives.

They are darkened in their understanding and separated from the life of God because of the ignorance that is in them due to the hardening of their hearts. (Ephesians 4:18)

Yet they say to God, "Leave us alone! We have no desire to know your ways." (Job 21:14)

Throughout the years I raised sheep, I was always able to identify *my* sheep the minute I stepped in the pasture. Only *my* sheep would make eye contact with me. Only *their* eyes would meet mine. And in that one second of eye contact, those little lambs would capture my heart every time!

Turn your eyes from me; they overwhelm me. (Song of Songs 6:5)

Their eyes would penetrate deep into mine; searching for a sign of my intent. When they realized I was approaching their fence line, they would take off running and start their ecstatic bouncing all along the fence; peering back at me every few seconds, fearful of losing me.

"Baa baa, baa baa" sounded like "mama, mama."

I knew they wanted to get through the fence and jump into my arms. They knew me. They knew my love. They trusted me. They wanted to be with me. They were my kids!

You can tell for sure that you are now fully adopted as his own children because God sent the Spirit of his Son into our lives crying out, "Papa! Father!" Doesn't that privilege of intimate conversation with God make it plain that you are not a slave, but a child? And if you are a child, you're also an heir, with complete access to the inheritance. (Galatians 4:6–7 MSG)

They were just a few, my adopted kids. And I ruined them! They would never again be content to spend the rest of their lives seeking food in Sheep World. They found something they wanted much more . . . their shepherd! They would spend the rest of their lives looking for me.

Then said I, "Woe is me! For I am undone and ruined, because I am a man of unclean lips, and I dwell in the midst of a people of unclean lips; for my eyes have seen the King, the Lord of hosts!" (Isaiah 6:5 AMP)

At first I felt bad that my sheep were experiencing such tension. They were constantly on alert, watching and listening for the sound of my voice or my entrance. It was caused by their fervent seeking for someone who was not in visual residence. Then I realized that balancing this tension was part of the higher life; it was a good thing. They never once became so involved with the other lambs or even their food that they missed my coming. If they weren't experiencing this tension, it would have meant something in Sheep World had replaced their first love.

The Shearing Shed

If we're not experiencing this type of tension between the two worlds, something is seriously wrong. If the Lord God is not first in our lives, an idol or a false god is taking his place—and we need to immediately fall flat on our faces before God and ask for his forgiveness!

When I entered the sheep pasture, the other sheep never looked up. They were so happy in their continuous consumption that they didn't need me. They had no idea how much I wanted them to just look up and acknowledge I was there. At least that would have been a start.

Father, I want those you have given me to be with me where I am, and to see my glory, the glory you have given me because you loved me before the creation of the world. (John 17:24)

The wonderful Australian electric fence system for sheep that Honey installed eliminated the need for me to stand guard over my sheep. Absolutely nothing could get in or out of that fence system. As a consequence, the other sheep still didn't know me. As long as this was the case, I would be spending all my days trying to care for blinded, self-sufficient sheep that fought me every inch of the way.

I longed to have all my sheep know my voice so they would follow me. Getting them to go anywhere was a nightmare. Instead of following me, they would scatter, each one going in a different direction. A five-minute excursion would turn into a frustrating thirty minutes.

> We all, like sheep, have gone astray,
> each of us has turned to his own way;
> and the LORD has laid on him
> the iniquity of us all. (Isaiah 53:6)

I started carrying a can of grain to get them to follow me. No matter how gently I shook the can, a wild, headlong rush of gluttonous animals would come stampeding toward me. Of course, they couldn't stop in time, and they would end up going around and ahead of me. Then they would panic and scatter because they didn't know where they were. I didn't consider these scenarios acceptable. There was only one way, the right way. These sheep needed to know their shepherd.

> As a shepherd seeks out his sheep in the day that he is among his flock that are scattered, so will I seek out My sheep; and I will rescue them out of all places where they have been scattered in the day of clouds and thick darkness. (Ezekiel 34:12 AMP)

Time was a precious commodity in my life; but I did find a way to spend more time with the sheep without taking time away from my family. This new discovery was called "early morning." I decided to spend my early mornings in the sheep pastures for the summer, so the indifferent sheep would get used to seeing me and hearing my voice. It would be a strategic time for these sheep. I hoped they would look up and acknowledge my presence!

The Lord was just waiting for me to give up a little so he could shower me with a lot! Numerous unexpected delights bombarded me as I dragged myself out of bed, sometimes grumbling, and made the trek to the pasture.

Shearing Shed

Sleeping in was one of many sheep behaviors of mine taken to the barn for shearing—ouch! Once the heavy weight of my woolly, self-indulgent sleep behavior was removed, I was set free to enjoy a new path of wonder and delight.

There were many mornings when I stood before my Shepherd with my share of problems, hurts, sins, failings, and ongoing trials. I wasn't all that brave either. I would envision my own sheep on the floor when I treated them . . . petrified, shivering, and afraid of pain. Somehow it encouraged me. Morning after morning I cried out, "Here I am again, Lord. Go ahead. Throw me down on the barnyard floor. Do whatever it is you have to do to me. Though I'm scared to death, I put my trust in you."

The first thing I discovered was the unspeakable beauty of the sunrise where I found the Son resides. Early morning in Sheep World was heavenly. I was sure the fiery red, orange, and golden threads that touched the tips of the trees were hand painted by God himself.

The unworldly mists spoke to me of the present veil between Sheep World and God's world, and as they slowly dissipated, I entered into his presence.

> In the morning, O Lord, you hear my voice;
> in the morning I lay my requests before you
> and wait in expectation. (Psalm 5:3)

Good Grain

Have you been snipped, dipped, clipped, and sheared? Adopted, adored, taught, and restored? Then you, too, are a sheep of his pasture.

Because of the Lord's great love we are not consumed, for his compassions never fail. They are new every morning; great is your faithfulness. I say to myself, "The Lord is my portion; therefore I will wait for him. The Lord is good to those whose hope is in him, to the one who seeks him. (Lamentations 3:22-25)

Jesus calls himself "the rising sun" and "the bright and morning star."

"The morning star" appears just before dawn when the night is cold and still very dark. When we are at our bleakest, lying on the cold shearing floor or feeling the painful snipping and clipping, Jesus will come to us with the warmth of his morning sun, filling us with light and truth. He is always faithful to come.

> Because of the tender mercy of our God, by which the rising sun will come to us from heaven to shine on those living in darkness and in the shadow of death, to guide our feet into the path of peace. (Luke 1:78–79)

The indifferent sheep did get comfortable seeing and hearing me that summer, and they finally came when I called them. They got it . . . I was there in their smelly pastures only to give them good things from my loving heart.

> This is how God showed his love among us: He sent his one and only Son into the world that we might live through him. This is love: not that we loved God, but that he loved us. (John 4:9–10a)

These sheep didn't have a close relationship with me like my orphans did, but if they continued to listen to my voice and follow after me, they could enter into their destiny.

> My sheep listen to my voice; I know them, and they follow me. I give them eternal life, and they shall never perish; no one can snatch them out of my hand. (John 10:27-28)

Chew on This

Before I even knew the Good Shepherd and began following him, he was there in my life . . . leading, guiding, and protecting me. He was always there. Like the complacent, need-nothing sheep, I just never looked up.

I have come to terms with being a sheep. I can't overemphasize how much freedom and security this truth has given me. I no longer deal with the burden of trying to control my life or others'. No matter what is happening, I am continually at peace because I know God is in charge. God is definitely God, and I am (thankfully) not. I am a happy sheep of his pasture.

> Know that the LORD is God. It is he who made us, and we are his; we are his people, the sheep of his pasture. (Psalm 100:3)

The Lord tells us in the Bible that the knowledge of who we are and who owns us is a prerequisite for entrance into his kingdom.

> Blessed are the poor in spirit, for theirs is the kingdom of heaven. (Matthew 5:3)

> Blessed (happy, to be envied, and spiritually prosperous—with life—joy and satisfaction in God's favor and salvation, regardless of their outward conditions) are the poor in spirit (the humble, who rate themselves insignificant), for theirs is the kingdom of heaven!" (Matthew 5:3 AMP)

> God blesses those people who depend only on Him. They belong to the kingdom of heaven! (Matthew 5:3 CEV)

Good Grain

The kingdom of heaven (also called the kingdom of God) is not a geographic place but a spiritual realm within every believer filled with the Holy Spirit. These believers cross all denominational and nondenominational lines and are from every nation on earth. They are called and have been given the authority to bring the kingdom of heaven to earth by doing the things that Jesus did. Jesus calls His spirit-filled believers his body, his church, and his sheep. (*Read the NIV commentary in Matthew 13:24.*)

Chew on This

The Beatitudes in the Bible also imply the enviable state of those who are filled with Christ's Spirit and have his mentality rather than a sheep's mentality. The Beatitudes contrast the values found in the Master's house with the values found in Sheep World. The Beatitudes describe how God's adopted and transformed sheep will live as they continue to mature and follow him. These sheep are not exempt from hooves to the head, rejection, or abuse; they experience a deeper form of happiness. They are "blessed." Webster's Dictionary tells us that to be blessed is to enjoy the bliss of heaven. The Shepherd's sheep are blessed no matter what happens to them in Sheep World.

The Beatitudes of the Bible:

Blessed are the poor in spirit,
> for theirs is the kingdom of heaven.
Blessed are those who mourn,
> for they will be comforted.
Blessed are the meek,
> for they will inherit the earth.
Blessed are those who hunger and thirst for righteousness,
> for they will be filled.
Blessed are the merciful,
> for they will be shown mercy.
Blessed are the pure in heart,
> for they will see God.
Blessed are the peacemakers,
> for they will be called sons of God.

Blessed are those who are persecuted because of righteousness,
    for theirs is the kingdom of heaven.

Blessed are you when people insult you, persecute you and
falsely say all kinds of evil against you because of me. Rejoice
and be glad, because great is your reward in heaven, for in the
same way they persecuted the prophets who were before you.
(Matthew 5:1–12, also read Luke 6:20–26)

The Shearing Shed

Lord, forgive me for not coming into your presence
frequently in praise and worship. Only there will my indifference be transformed into a fiery pursuit of you!

chapter twelve

OUR DESTINY

"No, Mom, no! Not Joey! You can't take Joey!"

"Mom, please let us have him for a pet. Please. We'll all help."

"We've been talking about this for weeks. I thought it was settled. This is why Joey was born . . . it's his destiny. And besides, he would be miserable as a pet. And we can't keep him as a ram and have him inbreeding the flock."

"No, I guess not."

"We would have to lock him in a stall away from the ewes, and you know he would hate that. He'd be one very lonely ram."

"We wouldn't let him get lonely, Mom."

"I know. I've been trying to think of a way to keep him too. I thought maybe we could castrate him, but he would still have to be isolated when the ewes were grained, and Milo told me he would get ugly after a while."

"Joey get ugly? Never!"

"I know how much you girls love him, and I do too."

"Then how can you do it, Mom? How can you take him to be . . ."

"Because I love the little guy, that's how. To keep him would be fun for us but not for Joey. After all he's been through, he deserves to come into his destiny. And besides, next spring I'm sure we'll have another orphan or two. Just remember, this isn't a petting zoo. It's a working farm. We're doing the right thing."

∽

"Honey, I sounded so strong and sensible this morning when I talked with the girls . . . and here I am, a mess!"

"You made the right decision, and I'm really proud of you."

"I'm out of Kleenex; can I borrow your handkerchief?"

"Look's like we'll be there any minute now, so get ahold of yourself. Here it is . . . the meat-packing house. Help me, now. The guy told me to drive around to the back and unload them in the pen back there. It's so dark, I can't see anything. Do you see a sheep pen anywhere?"

"There're some kind of animals over there . . . they look like hippopotamuses."

"Oh, they're hogs."

"They get that big? They're giants."

"I don't see any other pen back here. Now what do we do?"

"You're asking me? You're the fix-it-upper problem solver. Do your thing, Honey, and hurry. The sooner we get this terrible deed done, the better."

I felt like Honey and I were on a clandestine mission to do something very awful.

Honey grabbed a flashlight and a broken shovel handle from the trunk, climbed up on the pen, and analyzed the situation. The huge hogs had been left in an aisleway that led to three large, empty pens. Honey decided to use the shovel handle to coax the hogs into one of the pens so we could put our lambs in the other two. I was holding the flashlight for Honey, and he was doing the coaxing.

After about fifteen minutes I fled the scene. I jumped back in the car, rolled up the windows, slid down in my seat, closed my eyes, and held my ears. The sound coming from those monstrous hogs was worse than anything I had ever heard in my life. They were squealing and shrieking so loud I panicked. I was sure the police would screech in at any moment, and our covert operation would be exposed. I could just see the newspapers: "Local Couple Found Guilty . . . beating hogs and attempted first-degree murder of innocent lambs."

When Honey finally persuaded the last hog into the pen, the night became quiet again. I peered out the window and was relieved the police weren't there. I got out of the car to help unload our precious cargo. Honey never mentioned my escape.

Without speaking, we guided our immaculate, pampered lambs through the now pig-stenched aisleway and into one of the prison-like cells, I mean, stalls. The lambs were packed together like sardines and didn't move or make a sound. Their silence endeared them to me . . . which made me feel worse. They were so innocent.

We were ready to leave when we heard a little commotion. A lamb from the rear was pushing and shoving his way to the front. I was afraid to look. Sure enough, it was Joey. He looked me straight in the eye and didn't make a sound. I looked into his beautiful face and held his head with both of my hands and told him for the last time, "It's going to be okay, little guy."

I ran back to the car. There was no conversation going home . . . just sobs and Honey's respectful silence. No one asked us how it went that night, and I never spoke of it. No one really wants to face the poignant reality of an innocent lamb being slaughtered for our sake.

> He was led like a lamb to the slaughter, and as a sheep before her shearers is silent, so he did not open his mouth. (Isaiah 53:7b)

Losing Joey broke open that closed door on the subject of death, dying, purpose, and mankind's final destiny. It jolted all of us back into the "real" reality that we are only here to be transformed into the likeness of Jesus so we can fulfill our God-given purpose on earth, and at day's end, enter the kingdom of heaven.

Our first life-altering year of raising sheep was over. All the lambs went to the "market" in late spring, and the ewes remained with us. I so enjoyed watching the ewes peacefully grazing on our pastures, looking so beautiful, so English, and demanding absolutely nothing from us. It was pure bliss, just like it was that very first summer . . . that is until the ram came the following fall.

After the hard lessons of that first year, combined with the wisdom gained through four lambing seasons, trying out three feeding programs and two marketing plans, I finally found a plan that worked best for me. I wrote it up and would read it every so often to make sure I was staying on track. The following is the exact copy of my scribbled-out plan:

Shepherding:

I commit to take excellent care of every ewe in my flock until they reach the standard I have set for them.

I'll rotate them on four pastures with water in the summer and feed high-quality hay in the barn and paddock area for the winter. Administer or provide yearly vaccinations, shearing and treat injuries and diseases. (Study about new vaccinations.) I will cull every ewe that is not birthing twins, lacks mothering skills, is injured, or just never reaches my standard. (Al Dennie agreed to take my culled ewes to Clare's livestock auction.)

I will flush and breed standard-ready ewes with a ram that will upgrade my flock. (I need a higher leg conformation . . . an increase in the length as well as the thickness to the leg.)

Goal—Ewes to produce a 200 percent crop of lambs every year. (Twins for every ewe.) Bring them to market as quality-graded Prime or Choice Lamb at 110 pounds minimum by fifth or sixth month of age. The younger the lamb, the more tender it is. (Study and practice how to yield-grade them.)

I've chosen a lamb-feeding program that will allow the lambs to stay with their mothers until they go to market . . . nursing and grazing with their moms plus all the creep feed they can eat.

I believe the more content they are, the more they thrive. High quality creep feed from the grain elevator in Freeland is supplemented with enough vitamins and minerals.

Marketing:

I can't keep up with the constant fluctuation of the price of lamb, so instead of taking them to the market in Clare, I'll sell them to private buyers who will pay me for *one whole lamb*. The buyer will pick up their cut, wrapped, and frozen lamb according to their own specifications at the meat packing company of my choice. (Give them the phone number so they can call in their cutting and wrapping instructions.)

I'm satisfied with the private pricing arrangements and the cooperation of our hygienically clean meat-packing company. (They have window boxes filled with petunias and ivy—yes!)

The Lamb Education Center in Denver, Colorado sent me boxes of recipe books called *Lamb Around the World*. I will give every customer a book along with my best recipes and a short personal note.

Yes, our family now loves the special entrée . . . lamb. Our favorite recipe is a honey-mustard-glazed deboned leg of lamb slowly cooked on the rotisserie. Our second favorite is lamb chops grilled quickly, served with mint jelly. Our third favorite is a fruit-stuffed leg of lamb baked in the oven . . . or is it the fancy French rack of lamb with the rib ends covered with paper frills? Or the lamb roast baked slowly in the oven with pineapple, apricots, and spices with an aroma that calls everyone to the kitchen? Or maybe it's the delicious stuffed and rolled lamb shanks or the Oriental lamb stew that simmers all day. Then there is our famous Christmas crown roast of lamb stuffed with a cranberry and sweet cream dressing with pecans. Oh, I can't forget our end-of-the-summer dish: Turkish lamb and vegetable casserole made with ground lamb, fresh tomatoes, zuc-chini, green peppers, and little red potatoes.

The lambs were not born to live; they were born to die, so they could reach their destiny. Their ultimate purpose was not to take place in Sheep World but in their master's world, in our home. Only those lambs who reached my standard ended up on my table.

Jesus was not born to live; he was born to die for our sins and was raised to life for our justification so we could reach our destiny in the Shepherd's home.

He came down from heaven, entered our fallen world, died on the cross, resurrected, rose again from the dead, and was glorified, enabling us to believe and hope in him. Believers in Jesus Christ would become righteous, not by their works, but by his death on the cross. He died so that everyone on the earth could be included in his resurrection life.

> That if you confess with your mouth, "Jesus is Lord," and believe
> in your heart that God raised him from the dead, you will be
> saved. (Romans 10:9)

We were not born just to live; we were also born to die to self (the cross) and to be transformed into the likeness of Jesus Christ (our destiny)! Then we will fellowship with God, bring life to others, and enjoy life forever in his kingdom.

Do we want to die to ourselves? Of course we don't. We would just as soon remain stinking, selfish sheep. But when we put our focus and trust in Jesus and surrender our lives to him, it will just happen. Believe me, he will make sure of it.

Good friends of ours shared how they met Jesus and what happened when they gave their lives to him.

They both had good jobs, their kids were out of the house, and life was great. Every night after work they drove their baby blue Corvette to a nightclub and partied with their friends. They were living on easy street until their youngest son was tragically killed two weeks before his wedding. They were totally devastated. They hurt so badly they didn't know if they would make it.

After the funeral, a stranger approached their limousine and knocked on the window. Taken aback a little by this invasion of privacy, they courteously rolled the window down, and the woman slipped them a piece of paper with a phone number on it. She said, "If you don't know where to turn, call me."

They didn't know where to turn, and two weeks later they called her. The woman invited them to come to a Spirit-filled prayer meeting that met weekly. Desperate, they went. They were comforted by the peace and hope that filled the large room where a good number of praying people gathered to worship Jesus. They never planned to attend regularly, but every week they couldn't wait to get there. It wasn't long before both of them surrendered their lives to Jesus Christ.

As they tell the story, they never *decided* to die to self. They never agonized about giving up their martinis or partying with their friends. They were just so excited about Jesus and all they were learning about him, they forgot to go. They had found something better.

The Lord gave them good friends at that prayer meeting, and he gave them a wonderful new life. Today they are in Christian ministry and have been responsible for bringing many people to Jesus Christ.

> For if you live according to the sinful nature, you will die; but if by the Spirit you put to death the misdeeds of the body, you will live, because those who are led by the Spirit of God are sons of God. (Romans 8:13–14)

> Now if we are children, then we are heirs—heirs of God and co-heirs with Christ, if indeed we share in his sufferings in order that we may also share in his glory. (Romans 8:17)

Just as our adopted orphans had full access to everything we owned, so the Christian has full access to his Father's kingdom. The privileges and riches of the kingdom of God are spiritual and can only be received by a spiritual person in which the likeness of Jesus is present. Only as we become like Jesus will we be able to access and bring to earth the spiritual treasures of heaven and do the things that Jesus did. Warning: Focus on Jesus, not on the treasures!

For we who are alive are always being given over to death for Jesus' sake, so that his life may be revealed in our mortal body. (2 Corinthians 4:11)

The Shearing Shed

This couple put their trust in Jesus, and Sheep World, with its temporary and shallow treasures, faded out. Are we putting our trust in Jesus or the world? Are we building up our spiritual life or our carnal life? Are we accumulating spiritual truths or the barn's treasures? Choose Christ and watch your self die and come back to life . . . a new life in Christ. You'll be more alive, purposeful, and functioning when you are the person God created you to be.

Chew on This

Death is the destiny of every man; the living should take this to heart. (Ecclesiastes 7:2b)

If there was nothing beyond death, we could say, "Eat, drink martinis, and let's party, for tomorrow it's all over!" Christians believe there is a wonderful life beyond the grave and that life on earth is a preparation for eternal happiness with God.

Our present bodies are perishable and prone to decay. Our resurrection bodies will be transformed. These spiritual bodies will not be limited by the laws of nature. This does not necessarily mean we'll be super people, but our bodies will be different from and more capable than our present, earthly bodies. Our spiritual bodies will not be weak, will never get sick, and will never die. (See 1 Corinthians 15:42–44 MSG.)

> Jesus said to her, "I am the resurrection and the life. He who believes in me will live, even though he dies; and whoever lives and believes in me will never die. Do you believe this?" (John 11:25–26)

Our earth is not destined to live forever either; it too will eventually die.

When Jesus returns again, the earth will be judged by fire (Revelation 6:12–17). Scripture tells us God will create a new heaven and a new earth (2 Peter 3:7). *The Message* Bible calls it "The Day the Sky Will Collapse."

> Don't overlook the obvious here, friends. With God, one day is as good as a thousand years, a thousand years as a day. God isn't late with his promise as some measure lateness. He is restraining himself on account of you, holding back the End because he doesn't want anyone lost. He's giving everyone space and time to change. (2 Peter 3:8–9 MSG)

> And this gospel of the kingdom will be preached in the whole world as a testimony to all nations, and then the end will come. (Matthew 24:14)

Since everything here today might well be gone tomorrow, do you see how essential it is to live a holy life? Daily expect the Day of God, eager for its arrival. The galaxies will burn up and the elements melt down that day—but we'll hardly notice. (2 Peter 3:11–12 MSG)

Peter is telling us that those who are so in love with Jesus and so focused on him will hardly notice the sky is collapsing! Wow! That says a lot!

The Spirit of God whets our appetite by giving us a taste of what's ahead. He puts a little bit of heaven in our hearts so that we'll never settle for less. (Read 2 Corinthians 5:1-8 from *The Message*.)

At the very end of time, the Holy City, the New Jerusalem, will come down out of heaven from God, prepared as a bride for her husband. (Read Revelation 21.) Only those people whose names are written in the Lamb's Book of Life will be able to live there.

And I heard a loud voice from the throne saying, "Now the dwelling of God is with men, and he will live with them. They will be his people, and God himself will be with them and be their God. He will wipe every tear from their eyes. There will be no more death or mourning or crying or pain, for the old order of things has passed away." (Revelation 21:3–4)

Good Grain

Jesus will continue to shepherd us in our eternal home as found in Revelation 7:17, "For the Lamb at the center of the throne will be their shepherd; he will lead them to springs of living water. And God will wipe away every tear from their eyes."

Jesus is called (and is) our Good Shepherd and the holy Lamb of God. He leads and guides us now, and will continue to do so forever . . . in his home.

> Because the Lord is my shepherd, I have everything I need!
> He lets me rest in the meadow grass and leads me beside the quiet streams. He restores my failing health. He helps me do what honors him the most.
> Even when walking through the dark valley of death I will not be afraid, for you are close beside me, guarding, guiding all the way.
> You provide delicious food for me in the presence of my enemies. You have welcomed me as your guest; blessings overflow!
> Your goodness and unfailing kindness shall be with me all of my life, and afterwards I will live with you forever in your home.
> (Psalm 23 TLB)

part two

LIFE IN SHEEP WORLD

chapter thirteen

HEARTLAND FARM

Slowly, critter by critter, our farm expanded. Before we knew it, we were an old-fashioned working farm, raising all our own meat and eggs and growing our own vegetables. We topped our beds with wool-stuffed quilts and the cellar with potatoes, squashes, and apples. We opened the half acre of grapes for "U-Pick," and the girls showed their horses in 4-H. Honey was raising Herefords, and I was still shepherding sheep and planting gardens. We loved our farm projects, and we were enjoying the fruits of each other's labor.

Life was not without its share of problems and sufferings. All four of our daughters were diagnosed with mononucleosis within the first two years we lived on the farm, and they suffered frequent relapses for years. Honey's lifelong journey of pain from a spinal injury started about the same time. Both of us lost our fathers—one to cancer and the other to Alzheimer's—leaving both our mothers early widows. Despite the trials, we found life to be abundant and overflowing on the now-named "Heartland Farm."

I thought we were pretty normal farmers until our nearest neighbor commented, "You're the only farmer I know who vacuums her henhouse!"

We were also hearing similar comments from visitors; "Why, you could eat off the floor of this barn! Do I have to take my shoes off in here?"

Our daughters kept their horses, the stalls, and the whole

barn spotless. I guess our family hadn't quite shed their suburban expectations.

Before long we had three large gardens. Honey and I made a brightly colored, life-size scarecrow to adorn one. This smiling scarecrow had his head and his arms raised wide and high into the heavens, obviously praising the Lord with full abandon. He spoke of our hearts.

> But you are a chosen people, a royal priesthood, a holy nation, a people belonging to God, that you may declare the praises of him who called you out of darkness into his wonderful light. (1 Peter 2:9)

Jimmy's teacher from preschool called early one October morning.

"Hi! Is this Jimmy's mom?"

"Yes, is everything okay?"

"Well, kind of. You know the trip we planned to the dairy farm near Bay City?

"Yes."

Well, they just canceled it, and we wondered if we could bring the kids to your farm instead?

"Of course, I'd love it."

I woke up early and swept the walkway through the barn, shoveled out a couple of wheelbarrows of sheep pebbles, and tidied up the henhouse. The whole time I was cleaning up, I was trying to decide what I should do with the kids. What surprised me was how many choices I had. I decided I'd first let them hand-feed the sheep. I could just envision the kids giggling as the sheep mouthed their little hands clean. It really tickles. I started getting excited. Then I could put a bucket of grain on the ground in front of the kids and let them call the cows in. I mischievously smiled, knowing their eyes would pop out with terror when the docile but humongous cows headed for the bucket. I knew because I still felt shivers up and down my spine when they headed toward me. *And wait until they see the commotion the cows make trying to share one bucket. Hey, that would make a great lesson about sharing . . . I bet they'd never forget it either.*

I heard a horn honk. I ran to the road and directed the drivers to an area where they could park their cars . . . right across from the pond. I greeted the teachers and mothers with our 165-pound German shepherd, Christy, by my side. I asked them to keep their kids with them at all times. I noticed the parents' eyes appeared alarmed and were darting back and forth from the dog to the pond— and then each grabbed the hand of the nearest child and pulled him or her in close. I didn't mean to scare them. Three of the kids started crying and refused to get out of their cars. Now everyone seemed to be upset. I sensed the whole group was unsure about Christy. I didn't blame them for that; she was extra huge, even for a Shepherd, and she had a scary-looking black face. I brought Christy over to the cars and introduced her to each sobbing child and his or her upset parent and asked Christy to shake hands with them . . . and she offered her paw. I assured them that Christy loves kids and is as gentle as a lamb. As incredulous as this sounds, Christy smiled wide, beaming with happiness. She no longer looked scary but welcoming. It was a moment in time I will never forget. Every teacher, mother, and child shook Christy's paw that morning, and their faces reflected Christy's.

The group hadn't even left the car area when our pet turkey, Icobod, came waddling over and welcomed the group by gobbling right in their faces. Jimmy was yelling at the top of his voice with authority, "Don't be afraid! He won't hurt you!"

Jimmy stepped up to the plate and took complete control of the situation.

"Icobod likes kids. He even gives back rubs. Do you want one?"

Of course, all the kids yelled out yes! And then they started chanting, "We want a back rub! We want a back rub!"

The teachers looked confused, and before they could say anything, Jimmy was showing them how to get one.

"Do what I'm doing," he said.

He positioned himself facedown in the grass on his stomach and waited quietly. You could hear a pin drop. Sure enough, Icobod wobbled over to Jimmy and marched all over his back. Instantly every kid plopped himself down in the grass, though scared to death, and waited. Icobod didn't disappoint them and waddled from back to back, giving each one of them a good massage. Of course, they screamed and howled with laughter and would jump up and then back down again. They didn't want this bizarre experience to end.

"Jimmy, make Icobod do it again! Again! Again!"

The teachers, of course, were a wreck. They were wringing their hands and shaking their heads, and they kept looking at me to see if I approved, which I did, because I knew Icobod.

No one wanted to go home that day, and I didn't want them to leave. My first tour was a blazing success. The teachers asked the kids which animal they liked the best. Tony the Pony and Icobod were a tie. I innocently remarked to Jimmy's teacher, "The kids should have been here last spring when the barn was full of newborn lambs." That one remark completely restyled my entire life for the next fourteen years. I would soon be hosting a minimum of six hundred schoolchildren throughout the month of May. The schools would call for reservations the day after New Year's, and I would be booked up in a week. Every child would get a ride on Tony the Pony as I walked or jogged alongside them. That was my special time alone with each little person. I loved it. I also lost ten pounds by the end of May. It was a nice perk.

We opened our farm to Christian families for a Fourth of July Old-Fashioned Picnic. Invitation was by word of mouth. The number of families increased every year, reaching almost four hundred. The cars completely filled our largest horse pasture.

We had a women's prayer group that met in our home weekly for all the sixteen years we lived there. Eventually our husbands met in the evening. We became a real family. These godly brothers and sisters helped organize the large Christian picnics and served the people who came. They filled large water troughs with watermelons and ice, and they filled old-fashioned crocks up to the brim with lemonade. They organized a dozen old-time games, like potato-sack races and a tug-of-war over the pond. Kids and parents both participated. Each family brought a dish to pass around, and two Ping-Pong tables were occupied for hours. Every picnic ended with praise and worship around a large bonfire, often led by local church musicians. The picnickers would be declaring the glory of God within a five-mile radius through huge speakers set up on the old wraparound porch. We received unexpected reports of the "heavenly music" from our neighbors.

The pond was the focal point of every summer gathering. During the larger picnics, we assigned lifeguards at the pond, and we insisted the parents be with their children. The shallow end would be teeming with kicking and splashing arms and legs. Out in the deeper part, the older boys would be rocking the raft and fearlessly diving off the rocks. Honey and I would squeeze each other's shaky hands, silently praying for God's protection. God was faithful. In all those years, not one person was ever injured.

"Because he loves me," says the LORD, "I will rescue him; I will protect him, for he acknowledges my name. He will call upon me, and I will answer him; I will be with him in trouble, I will deliver him and honor him." (Psalm 91:14–15)

We ended up having picnics for an amazing variety of people. We hosted whole-church picnics, church youth groups, senior groups, hearing- and seeing-impaired groups, homeschool groups, inner-city schools, and of course, our own family gatherings.

What our family was doing seemed to be the natural thing to do. It was easy. We were just living out our assignment from the Lord for that particular season of our lives. We were given his grace, so it wasn't a burden but a joy. There is nothing better in the whole world than to be in the center of God's will.

> Now may the God of peace [Who is the Author and the Giver of peace], Who brought again from among the dead our Lord Jesus, that great Shepherd of the sheep, by the blood [that sealed, ratified] the everlasting agreement (covenant, testament), strengthen (complete, perfect) and make you what you ought to be and equip you with everything good that you may carry out His will; [while He Himself] works in you and accomplishes that which is pleasing in His sight, through Jesus Christ (the Messiah); to Whom be the glory forever and ever (to the ages of the ages). Amen (so be it). (Hebrews 13:20–21 AMP)

Raising a flock of sheep became a normal and satisfying part of my busy life. Shepherding didn't steal from my life but enhanced it. Having to run out to the barn to feed an orphan wasn't an interruption but a gift of peace and quiet. I could actually feel the tension in my body dissipate as I watched little droplets of milk fall from the chin of a lamb slurping his bottle. It was my quiet time, holding the bottle, caught up in the emerging truths that were everywhere in Sheep World.

Remembering the scenes around me during feeding times brings forth such vivid paintings in my memory that I wonder if I am not really there again, marveling. I remember sunny spring days with little lambs napping on the full-wool backs of their mothers; others trying to walk on their mothers' backs, falling, then bouncing right back up again. *Are they playing King of the Mountain?* No matter what their antics, the mother's rhythmic chewing of cud would never lose a beat. It was almost comical.

I remember seeing piles and piles of sleeping lambs pressed against each other and the sun-warmed silo in early spring, while their moms grazed together, "out for lunch." They were so intertwined, they looked like one large woolen quilt. It was fun to watch one of the quilt pieces wake up, stretch, and gently walk on top of the others to get to his mom.

I can still remember the unique tone and pitch of many of my ewes' baas. It amazed me that I knew so many of their voices and yet how few of them knew mine. I wasn't the only one who recognized the unique voices of sheep. Jimmy would come into the house, bleating in imitation of Pearl or Big Gracie, and would ask us to guess who it was. And we could! As he got older, he could imitate their bodily stances, the way they chewed, sniffed, or responded to grain. He would have us laughing so hard we'd be crying.

The most amazing scene in Sheep World took place in the spring, when the newborn lambs would get together and do the "wave." They would gather at the top of the highest hill and in unison, run up and down, zigzagging; like a flock of birds, they never broke formation. We've seen the lambs keep this game going for as long as thirty minutes. They played like kids do all over the world.

God made these sheep for his glory and for the pleasure of man. Some days I couldn't stop marveling at his creation, his gifts; they were everywhere, for his people.

> The meadows are covered with flocks and the valleys are mantled with grain; they shout for joy and sing . . . Shout with joy to God, all the earth! Sing the glory of his name; make his praise glorious! Say to God, "How awesome are your deeds! So great is your power that your enemies cringe before you." (Psalm 65:13, 66:1–3)

Lambs are precious. They are meek and mild and exemplify innocence and a purity that is beyond us. God the Father chose the perfect name for his only Son, Jesus, "the Lamb of God" (John 1:29). John tells us in Revelation 5:6, "Then I saw a Lamb, looking as if it had been slain, standing in the center of the throne, encircled by the four living creatures and the elders."

I believe the depth of our ability to comprehend the innocence of a lamb depends upon our familiarity with them. Let me tell you a little story that happened when Jimmy was in kindergarten.

As soon as I heard Jimmy's school bus coming down the road, Tinkerbell and I took off running. We arrived at the end of our driveway just in time to see the bus come to a stop. The door opened, and as Jimmy started to come down the steps, the bus driver lady knocked him aside, passed him, ran toward me, and swooped up my lamb. Crazy thoughts instantaneously entered my mind. *She's kidnapping my lamb! Maybe there's a fire on the bus? No, she's got my lamb!* This out-of-the-box incident startled me.

The lady nestled the lamb under her chin, pushed her face deep in the wool at the lamb's neck, and in an exaggerated way, began smelling and caressing the newborn in a way only an old shepherd would do. Muffled by the wool and her tears, I heard bits and pieces of what she was saying, though she never looked my way.

"I . . . haven't held . . . orphan . . . was . . . a kid . . . not supposed . . . leave . . . bus . . . only take . . . one second . . . had to do it."

Then, incredulously, this large woman sprinted back to the bus, jumped in, shut the door, and took off like a drag racer, making up for lost time.

This woman had obviously spent quality time with lambs and comprehended their preciousness and innocence.

Several priests and Levites asked John the Baptist who he was. He confessed freely that he wasn't the Christ. Then the Pharisees asked John why he baptized people if he wasn't the Christ or Elijah or the Prophet. I love John's reply:

"I baptize with water," John replied, "but among you stands one you do not know. He is the one who comes after me, the thongs of whose sandals I am not worthy to untie." (John 1:26–27)

The next day John saw Jesus coming toward him and said, "Look, the Lamb of God, who takes away the sin of the world!" (v. 29)

Good Grain

John the Baptist comprehended the unearthly inno-cence and purity of Jesus and called him "the Lamb of God." In the presence of such heavenly innocence, John recognized his unworthiness and knew exactly where he came from.

He must become greater; I must become less. The one who comes from above is above all; the one who is from the earth belongs to the earth, and speaks as one from the earth. (John 3:30-31)

I discovered shepherding was a wonderful way to exercise and lose weight . . . which was important because I love to bake all kinds of sweet concoctions. I no longer endured boring treadmills and dumb-bells; instead, I had versatile workouts in the sheep pens, paddocks, and rolling pastures. I didn't have to lift weights, because a bucket of water in each hand built enough arm muscle for any woman. Just ask our beautiful daughters. No one could beat them in arm wrestling . . . male or female.

My daily workout schedule consisted of raking up the littered sheep paddock every morning before visitors arrived and of throwing those hundred-plus pounds of sheep on the floor for constant hoof trimming and exams. I also put in hours of brisk walking while leading the sheep to their different pastures.

During lambing season our family kept the lambing pens tidy by laying clean straw over the soiled straw. When the season was over, the pens were a good three feet deep. Every spring we worked together to empty out these beautifully cushioned lambing pens. This job usually lasted three days and guaranteed an all-over workout and substantial weight loss.

I could also count on losing a good five pounds when I joined the family baling hay in the summer. It is traditional to cut and bale hay on the hottest days in summer, as wet hay will mold and can cause serious problems for sheep and horses. For some reason our family loved "hay time." Even our teens would cancel their plans when the hay was ready. They sounded so excited about it that their guy friends often offered to help.

The trip back to the barn on the hay wagon after picking up a load of hay was definitely the high point of this job. Riding up high on unstable bales was just dangerous enough to make it exciting, yet at the same time it was soothing and restful as the hot breezes dried our wet bodies. There is something exhilarating about resting on top of a few hours of hard work.

Even though ice-cold lemonade waited for us back at the barn, we were always sad when the wagon pulled in. After downing the lemonade, someone would always pull out the hose and water down whomever they could reach; of course, they loved the high-pitched shrieks and screams. But when we heard the grinding clatter of the hay elevator running again, everyone stopped playing and silently headed back to work. It was Honey's way of saying, "The party's over."

The wet crew would break into three teams. Team one brought down the high bales from the hay wagon. Team two put them on the hay elevator, and Team three stacked them high in the one-hundred-plus-degree hayloft. Team one joined Team three up in "the oven" once they brought down the highest bales.

Our two youngest kids wanted to be as "strong and tough" as the rest of the family and begged Honey to let them work up in the hayloft. Honey never said no, but every year he had them try out for the job. He told them if they could catch a bale coming off the elevator, they'd have the job. Every year we winced as the bale would knock them flat on the ground. Everyone just loved on them and told them how important it was to load up the elevator and sweep up the loose hay. Honey always told them, "Maybe next year."

Honey was in charge of the hardest job, which was throwing or carrying the bales up in the hayloft and stacking them evenly so they wouldn't collapse. Of course, this is the job the teenage boys wanted to do—to show off for the girls. (That's when *I* winced.) Every year the guys were completely spent after one hour, while our girls could continue throwing those seventy-five- to one-hundred-pound bales around for hours.

I think hay time was enjoyable to us because someone was always joking around and laughing about, well, everything, and because we experienced a strong sense of belonging. We were a family. Setting up a year's supply of food for our animals also gave us a good feeling of accomplishment.

These were just some of the personalized workouts included in my shepherd's "ewe-aerobics." Very few people wanted to join my program.

Yes, I loved all those nincompoop sheep! I loved everything about them: the work, the surprises, and of course, the revelations I received.

It was in this setting on our now-named Heartland Farm that the following sheep stories took place.

chapter fourteen

THE LAMBSICLES

An upsetting sound of full-throated baa-ing coming from the sheep barn took me away from breakfast dishes. Alarmed, I sprinted out to the freezing barn without my coat to find Molly thrashing around in the larger lambing pen. She was invading the boundary of every ewe and checking out the scent of their lambs. The ewes were kicking at her and propelling straw everywhere while bleating so loud it hurt. They were probably yelling, "Red alert! Red alert! Mad Molly can't find her babies and wants ours!"

Molly was bleeding and dragging remnants of afterbirth behind her—but where were her lambs? I looked into the lambing pens and couldn't see any extras. I looked outside in the sheep paddock, which adjoins the warmer lambing pens, and there they were. Two frozen newborn lambs half-covered with bloodstained snow. Their blue-gray frozen tongues were protruding from their mouths and colored the whole macabre scene with a hopeless finality. The consistent expectancy of new life that I carried within me during lambing season took a piercing blow at that moment. At first it sickened me, but then anger rose up, and I yelled out, "No! In the name of Jesus, death, you will not have your way!"

Jane heroically gave up her "getting beautiful before school" time to help me with the lambs. I knew I couldn't do it alone. I gave Jane the game plan as we ran through the snow to the barn, "We're going to bring these little lambs back to life!" It sounded as crazy to me as I perceived it did to Jane.

We arrived at the crime scene and scooped up the frozen bodies. As we ran the two hundred feet back to the house, I wondered
if what I had read in *The Shepherd* magazine to revive cold lambs
would work for lambs that were frozen solid. It didn't matter. It was
the only thing I knew to do.

"Jane, if we move fast enough, you won't miss your bus. What
we're going to do is fill the laundry tub with warm water, immerse
the lambs, except for their noses, and slowly add hot water until our
hands can't stand it."

I loved how I sounded, like a doctor giving orders to her nurse.

"Hold on to the head with one hand, and two of the legs with
the other. Keep the nose out of the water!"

I actually sounded as though I knew what I was doing, but my
trembling-all-over body exposed the truth. Looking at the two frozen lambs bobbing in the water caused a wave of doubt and unbelief
to sweep through my mind. *These lambs are dead, frozen dead, and
now they're melting! What am I doing?*

The scene was bizarre, almost comical. Their little bodies were
thawing out fast, and they were floating to the top of the water
sideways. We were trying to keep them under water except for
their noses, but they kept floating up. As their limbs thawed, they
became slippery and felt like they were stretching. An image of the
old comic strip character Plastic Man came into my mind's view.
Now, that is old!

"Mom . . . this isn't working!"

Jane sensed the futility in our attempt.

"We can do it, Jane! Hang on to her! Keep her nose out of the
water! Let's give them a few more minutes. Turn the hot water on
again! Keep her underwater!" My faith was back, and I believed.

Then I felt my lamb take on substance. What an incredible feeling . . . life. About the same time, Jane yelled out, "Mom! I think
this lamb is alive!"

All at once their lifeless, slippery limbs began to feel muscular and in the right proportions. Then they began kicking like crazy as they were taking in deep breaths and expelling accumulated mucus rapidly.

"Mom, they're choking!"

"Just as fear was creeping up my back, both lambs started breathing normally. My right hand was holding the lamb right where her heart was, and suddenly I could feel her heart beating so fast I thought it would jump right out of her chest. At the same time her eyes opened, startled. I looked over at Jane . . . both lambs were alive!

We didn't have time to revel in the moment. We pulled them out of the water, wrapped them in big, fluffy towels, leaving their noses exposed, and deposited them in front of the heat register in the kitchen. Our dog immediately snuggled up to the two bundles and smelled their noses. Jane and I were exclaiming happy little phrases like, "Do you believe it?"

"Oh my gosh, they're alive!"

"Is this a miracle or what?"

"Look at them; they're so cute!"

Jane ran up the stairs, taking two steps at a time. Her sisters were already screaming, "The bus is almost here! Hurry! Hurry!"

Jane made a quick check in the kitchen before flying out the front door, and at that very moment, one of the lambs spoke: "Baa."

Jane looked up at me; our eyes met; words were unnecessary.

Before I could get the kitchen cleaned up, first one, then the other, almost simultaneously walked right out of their towels and instinctively began looking for their mother. The dog ignored their attempts to nurse and began to lick them, first one, then the other, just as their mother would have done. They stood still, totally entranced by this comforting experience.

Licking stimulates the flow of blood in a newborn and warms the body temperature. It removes any smell of afterbirth left from the birthing process, which could attract predators. It is pleasurable and comforts the lamb. It is during this time the ewe and her lamb begin talking to each other, establishing their relationship forever, by voice and by smell.

I knew Molly would never accept these twins. They had been bathed, and now they smelled like our dog: a sheep's natural predator.

I don't know why I took them out to the barn. I guess I had to actually see Molly reject them before I took them back into the house.

As I entered, I pressed the twins unusually close to my body, comforting them for their ensuing loss. It was quiet. I expected to see Molly still raising a ruckus. I peered into the larger lambing pen and saw a ewe licking a newborn lamb. It looked like Molly, but it couldn't be! I ran around the barn like a crazy lady counting my sheep. Sure enough, it was Molly! I had just missed the delivery of her third lamb by minutes. Noting the time lapse between the twins and this third lamb, I realized she had endured a difficult delivery without a shepherd's help. But she did it, and the lamb looked okay.

I knew exactly what to do, although I had never done it before. I whispered a thank-you to the Lord for my shepherding magazines. I went into the pen with the nicely bathed twins and began rubbing the newborn's afterbirth all over them. I was so excited it didn't even register what I was doing. I set the messy twins down next to baby number three, unplugged Molly's teats, and waited for the flow of colostrum. I left the pen and watched a real-life miracle unfold for the second time that morning.

Molly slowly spun around, licking one, then another, nudging one to come closer, checking out all their parts, all the while "talking" to her messy new triplets. She had two girls, and baby number three was a boy. He nursed first. Molly didn't let him nurse long, as she was still in a spinning mode, perhaps overcome that she had three babies. She finally settled down and nudged each lamb to her to nurse. I stayed as a witness until all three had little round tummies full of warm colostrum.

~

I was mopping up the water in the laundry room when it hit me. They had been dead, and now they were alive! I began laughing.

> Where, O death, is your victory? Where, O death, is your sting? (1 Corinthians 15:55)

Good Grain

Central to Christianity is the fact that Jesus literally died and rose again from the dead on the third day! Jesus defeated death for us!

> "I am the resurrection and the life. He who believes in me will live, even though he dies; and whoever lives and believes in me will never die. Do you believe this?" (John 11:25–26)

Do we believe it? I guess everyone needs to see and hear about people being raised from the dead and other powerful miracles, so we can believe that Jesus Christ really was victorious over death, that Jesus Christ really is the Son of God, filled with his Father's glory!

> "Do not believe me unless I do what my Father does. But if I do it, even though you do not believe me, believe the miracles; that you may learn and understand that the Father is in me, and I in the Father." (John 10:37–38)

> Don't ever forget the wonderful fact that Jesus Christ was a Man, born into King David's family; and that he was God, as shown by the fact that he rose again from the dead. (2 Timothy 2:8 TLB)

Chew on This

I looked up "miracles" in the chain index in the back of my Bible. There were pages of them listed. What is wrong with us Christians today?

In solemn truth I tell you, anyone believing in me shall do the same miracles I have done, and even greater ones, because I am going to be with the Father. You can ask him for anything, using my name, and I will do it, for this will bring praise to the Father because of what I, the Son, will do for you. Yes, ask anything, using my Name, and I will do it! (John 14:12–14 TLB)

I believe that Jane and I had been practicing our faith that morning, for a soon-to-be day.

chapter fifteen

THE FLOCK BOOK

People often asked us if we named our sheep. I had to answer yes. We used names instead of numbers because we were in conversation about our sheep every day, and referring to numbers just didn't work for us. We also ear punched their registered number for identification.

"Number 18 has a fever and should be checked out," would not get the same response as, "Big Gracie has a fever!"

If our Gracie did have a fever, we would all yell out, "No! No! Not ole Gracie!"

And everyone would take off running to the barn.

Naming the sheep became an enjoyable ongoing family project, kind of like a table puzzle. We tried not to use our relatives' or our friends' names, and with our large family, somebody always knew someone with the name we wanted. Sometimes the names fit our sheep too well!

We considered every name important because our sheep had now joined all the other components in our lives that were impacting our evolvement. We would never forget the names of the sheep that brought us spiritual revelation or revealed our sin, or those that were just so darn cute they would make us smile. The cute award definitely went to Sammy and Susan . . . twin koala bear look-alikes who made you melt as you looked into their large, dark eyes.

Look up into the heavens! Who created all these stars? As a shepherd leads his sheep, calling each by its pet name, and counts them to see that none are lost or strayed, so God does with stars and planets! (Isaiah 40:26 TLB)

It is very important for a shepherd to keep accurate records of everything that happens to every sheep. These records are kept in a flock book drawn up for every breed. During the lambing season I carried a pocket flock book around with me twenty-four hours a day. I remember being frustrated because everything I wore had to have pockets.

It was actually a bona fide miracle that I recorded anything at all, because at the peak of the lambing season, everything is very chaotic. There are ewes and babies bleating for help and others eerily quiet, needing to be buried. Entering precise information in the flock book often felt like the last straw. It was a painful discipline for me.

If I had known I would be reading through my flock books years later to resurrect sleeping memories for a book, I would have added more juicy details. I would also have washed my hands and used decipherable and coherent handwriting. I suspect my hands were coated with all that birthing stuff.

As soon as a ewe gave birth, I would look in the flock book for her breed of sheep and find her name. It would be found next to the flock number column, where her registered number is recorded along with the date she was bred, the sire, and his name and registered number. Next I would record the number of lambs she dropped; the date of their birth; and for each lamb, ram, and ewe, a weight and flock number. At the bottom of each page was a space to record remarks. I recorded everything I knew about their birth experience . . . if they were accepted or rejected, if they were with their moms or with us, and those who didn't make it at all. Of course, I jotted down all the great and interesting data . . . like miracle births, really cute markings, and unusual colorings. I also included all the terrible things that happened.

⌣

Once, a first-time mother easily delivered a set of twins and began the normal process of licking and cleaning them up. I did notice she was going at it very vigorously, but I left her to help another ewe that was going into labor. About fifteen minutes later the girls started screaming. They found the ewe still licking one of the twins, and his right ear was missing. By the time I arrived, most of his tail was gone and she was working on his other ear. We tried to stop her. We took her lambs out of the pen, but when we returned them she continued where she left off. The girls and I were holding our stomachs, walking back and forth, feeling nauseated. We were witnessing a heinous and beastly thing.

We called for Honey, who took one look and left to call our veterinarian. Honey came back with a can of black gooey tar and he did as he was instructed: he painted the tips of the lamb's protruding body parts with tar. Yes, tar, and it worked. It stopped the ewe from her carnivorous cleaning campaign, but it hurt to look at the poor little lamb. It was heartbreaking. The kids and I pampered our disfigured little guy like he was a celebrity. I'm sure he knew he was special. After he healed, the kids lovingly named him "Chewy." Chewy was one of our most pampered lambs, though he continued to stay with his mama.

Chew on This

Bad things happen to innocents in Sheep World . . . just because it is inhabited with sheep. Remember, life in Sheep World is temporary. For God's sheep—you and me—the best is yet to come!

God chose the weak things of the world to shame the strong. He chose the lowly things of this world and the despised things—and the things that are not—to nullify the things that are, so that no one may boast before him. (1 Corinthians 1:27-29)

Rarely did we name and record a newborn on the spot. It usually took us weeks to name our lambs. I remember spending about a month leafing back through my messy flock books to add names and updated information. But every name and all the pertinent information of every sheep in my flock was recorded in the book.

I had a flock book for every breed of sheep. In the front of each book is a list of the particular breeds' standards, with a scale of points. The Suffolk sheep's standard is as follows: the head gets twenty-five points if it is hornless, the face is black and long with a good hair coat, and the muzzle moderately fine and free of wrinkles. A small quantity of clean white wool on the forehead is not objected to. Ears must be a medium length, black in color with a fine texture that tips out at the end, and the eyes must be bright and full.

The neck receives five points if it is of moderate length and well set. In rams it should be stronger.

The back / loin receives twenty points if it is long, level, and well covered with meat and muscle. The tail must be broad and well set up, the ribs long and well sprung. The list goes on, reaching one hundred points. It is by this standard that each sheep is show-judged, while every shepherd has his own standard according to the purposes he has for his flock.

By keeping a record of the strong and weak points in my flock, I was able to know which areas needed help. For example: if my sheep had low points on the Back and Loin Standard, I would want to bring in a breeding ram that is strong in that area. This is called crossbreeding. A flock that doesn't crossbreed with other flocks will get weaker with each succeeding generation.

Sheep that have a very low point of standard must be culled from the flock. Culled sheep are normally taken to the slaughterhouse.

The Shearing Shed

The same is true in the church. If the church doesn't have connections and interchange with other believers and churches that are different, it will get weaker as time goes on. Inbreeding is definitely a sheep behavior that must go to the shearing shed!

A similar register is kept of the names of the people who are promised heavenly citizenship! Scripture tells us these names are also written in a book. This book is referred to as "the Lamb's Book of Life."

> Nothing impure will ever enter it [heaven], nor will anyone who does what is shameful or deceitful, but only those whose names are written in the Lamb's book of life. (Revelation 21:27)

There is a standard written in God's Word, the Bible. This standard must be met to have one's name written in the Lamb's Book of Life. That standard is righteousness. It is a spiritual standard that comes from God by our faith in Jesus Christ, wherein we believe that through his death on the cross and his resurrection from the dead, our sins are forgiven and we are made righteous. We can never attain this righteousness by ourselves.

We give Jesus our sins and he gives us his righteousness and forgiveness.

> God made him who had no sin to be sin for us, so that in him we might become the righteousness of God. (2 Corinthians 5:21)

Can a sheep attain the status of humanity by attempting to copy our behavior? It would be impossible. If the sheep continued to try, he would end up feeling guilty and condemned.

> I consider everything a loss compared to the surpassing greatness of knowing Christ Jesus my Lord, for whose sake I have lost all things. I consider them rubbish, that I may gain Christ and be found in him, not having a righteousness of my own that comes from the law, but that which is through faith in Christ—the righteousness that comes from God and is by faith. (Philippians 3:8–9)

Good Grain

Our Shepherd has also set his standard for the righteous sheep, based on the high purposes he has for them. He tells us in Matthew 25 that his standard is love in action . . . a concrete response to people in need. Because Jesus assumed our humanity, whatever we now do for the least of our brothers, we are doing for him.

The people that meet the Shepherd's standard by loving others prove they are his followers (his sheep). He will allow them to remain in his flock to reproduce this love that comes from him. The people who do not meet his standard will be removed from his flock . . . they will be culled. A people who fulfill the high purpose of loving God above all else and unconditionally loving their neighbor will be the Shepherd's glory.

> All the nations will be arranged before him and he will sort the people out, much as a shepherd sorts out sheep and goats, putting sheep to his right and goats to his left.

Then the King will say to those on his right, "Enter, you who are blessed by my Father! Take what's coming to you in this kingdom. It's been ready for you since the world's foundation." And here's why:

> I was hungry and you fed me,
> I was thirsty and you gave me a drink,
> I was homeless and you gave me a room,
> I was shivering and you gave me clothes,
> I was sick and you stopped to visit,
> I was in prison and you came to me.'

Then those "sheep" are going to say, "Master, what are you talking about? When did we ever see you hungry and feed you, thirsty and give you a drink? And when did we ever see you sick or in prison and come to you?" Then the King will say, "I'm telling the solemn truth: Whenever you did one of these things to someone overlooked or ignored, that was me—you did it to me.'

Then he will turn to the "goats," the ones on his left, and say, "Get out, worthless goats! You're good for nothing but the fires of hell. And why? Because—

> I was hungry and you gave me no meal,
> I was thirsty and you gave me no drink,
> I was homeless and you gave me no bed,
> I was shivering and you gave me no clothes,
> sick and in prison, and you never visited."
> (Matthew 25:31–43 MSG)

The Shearing Shed

We will be recognized as the sheep of his pasture by our love . . . by our loving response to people in need. But beware, if our number-one goal is not our relationship with Jesus Christ, our good deeds could puff us up and cause us to primp and prance around our puny performances!

The great triumph is not in your authority over evil, but in God's authority over you and presence with you. Not what you do for God but what God does for you—that's the agenda for rejoicing. (Luke 10:20 MSG)

Good Grain

The Lord's sheep are agents, ambassadors, and channels for his love. We are his heart, his hands, his mouthpiece, and his feet. Every time we are a participant of his eternal circle of passionate love—flowing in us, through us, back to him, and out to others—our spiritual DNA is being changed. Our response to him will become more like his and less like sheep. From baaaaa to yaaaaa.

And this is love: that we walk in obedience to his commands. As you have heard from the beginning, his command is that you walk in love. (2 John 1:6)

chapter sixteen

FOOT ROT

The first time I heard of the existence of the common sheep disease "foot rot," I think I was morbidly intrigued. It sounded so horrendously repulsive and frightening to me that I had to immediately find out how I could prevent this disgusting disease from contaminating my flock. The very worst words in man's vocabulary come under the description of rot: putrid, pustular, decomposing, fetid, festering, rank, foul, noxious, decaying, infectious, and deteriorating. Not good!

Foot rot is a highly contagious disease causing severe lameness in sheep. It is primarily an invasion of the sheep's hoof, and the infection spreads rapidly throughout the horny tissue. There is a foul characteristic discharge. The hoof growth becomes grotesquely distorted, and sheep will put little or no weight on an affected foot.

In severe outbreaks, it may affect up to 75 percent of a flock at one time. Once a sheep catches this disease, the infection may persist for years. Infected sheep will contaminate their pasture and every area where they have walked, so the disease spreads. Complete control can seldom be accomplished in one season and requires a carefully planned inspection program for several years. Foot rot is one of the most costly sheep diseases in labor, equipment, and materials.

The *Sheepman's Production Handbook* spelled out the nasty conditions that could spawn this creepy disease:

The organisms causing foot rot require an oxygen-deficient environment for growth. Therefore, overgrown, rolled-under hooves in wet, muddy, unsanitary conditions provide an excellent environment for these organisms. The well-worn or trimmed hoof is seldom affected.

Our sheep were living on uncontaminated pastures in sheep paradise. We were consistently trimming our sheep's hooves. Honey built our paddocks on clean, well-drained, sandy soil, and we were constantly maintaining their sanitary and well-ventilated housing. We knew our sheep wouldn't and couldn't ever get the frightful foot rot!

> Do not boast about tomorrow, for you do not know what a day may bring forth. (Proverbs 27:1)

For five years our sheep remained as pure and clean as snow! Foot rot became a long-ago-imagined battle to fight that never came; it was completely gone from our consciousness.

We had made the trip across the state to look at a beautiful registered Suffolk ram that was for sale. The ram was perfect for our flock of ewes but, of course, he cost twice as much as we wanted to spend. I placed a lower bid for him over the phone, and then I waited.

Our sixth flushing season was almost over, and we still hadn't heard if our bid was accepted. Then the phone call came . . . we did not get the ram. It was not only a disappointment, but I hadn't made any other arrangements for a ram—thanks to my presumption and a hundred and one other things I had to do before school started.

I needed a ram right away, like yesterday! I would have to forget my grand plan to breed my flock with a big-time stud and find a run-of-the-mill ram. I knew Milo would be using his best rams for his many flocks, but I hoped that maybe, just maybe, he could help me out, or knew someone who could.

He told me to call a shepherd named Maynard from the town north of us. Maynard said he was replacing one of his old Suffolk rams with a young ram, and he hadn't taken him to market yet. He was sure this old guy could still do his job and would give me good quality lambs.

To my delight, the sheep farmer personally delivered his old ram that very evening. I could barely make out his presence as he disappeared into the far end of the pasture where the ewes most likely stood. I emphatically thanked my rescuer, and life in my neck of the sheep-woods was good again.

All of our ewes conceived, and with one month to go, they were expanding dramatically. I didn't mind the unseasonably warm winter we were having because it enabled the expectant ewes to roam the snowless pastures, which kept them in good condition.

I was sipping my coffee one morning and mulling over my calendar when I spotted the ewes heading down the rolling pasture.

What? Something must be wrong on the hill . . . all of them are stumbling. They almost look like they're limping. Noooooooooo! They are limping!

Yes, it was foot rot. The old ram brought it in and defiled our spotless, unsullied, lily-white ewes and contaminated our unsoiled pastures. This was a devastating and shocking tragedy.

Chew on This

Foot rot is synonymous with the sin and evil that entered our world!

God created earth to be a wonderful place for his creatures to live . . . a literal paradise. Scripture tells us evil came to God's beautiful creation and tempted the first man and woman to rebel against God. When they made the decision to disobey God's commands and do what they wanted to do, the foul infection fully entered them.

Adam and Eve tried to hide their sin from God and even tried to hide it from themselves, making excuses and blaming each other rather than admitting the truth. Concealing sin, like foot rot in an oxygen-deficient environment, will allow the infection to spread. And spread it would. Every human being on earth would catch the infectious, rotting disease except God's Son, Jesus Christ.

But God had a plan that would overcome the effects of man's rebellion. The Bible is the unfolding story of this awesome plan . . . leading to God's visit to earth through his Son, Jesus Christ. Through the death of Jesus, God was able to forgive man for his sins and cleanse and restore him from his foul disease, forever.

The blood of Jesus, his Son, purifies us from all sin (1 John 1:7)

For the wages of sin is death, but the free gift of God is eternal life through Jesus Christ our Lord. (Romans 6:23 TLB)

The Shearing Shed

God is a holy God and hates sin! He knows that unless our sin is uncovered, it will fester, distort, corrupt, spread like a cancer, and eventually kill us! The infection of sin distorts man's beauty and his environment. It emits a foul-smelling identity that repulsively invades all boundaries. It is the smell of deterioration and death. Unless sinful man acknowledges his sin and submits to his Shepherd, he will not get trimmed, treated, or moved to a clean pasture where he can heal.

∽

I dove into my books, handbooks, and magazines, looking for information about foot rot. Australian sources reported good results when the shepherds vigorously trimmed the feet of infected sheep and treated them with a 10cc injection of penicillin-streptomycin and gave them a disinfectant footbath. We trimmed their obnoxious, diseased feet and gave them their injections immediately, working late into the night.

> From the sole of your foot to the top of your head there is no soundness—only wounds and welts and open sores, not cleansed or bandaged or soothed with oil. (Isaiah 1:6)

The next day we tackled the lengthy instructions on mixing a footbath solution and making the foot bath itself. The sheep would have to be forced to walk through a disinfectant bath of copper sulfate, formaldehyde, hydroxymethyl, nitro, propanediol, and iodophor concentrate. It seemed to me the concoction we were putting together was as obnoxious and foul smelling as the infection we were treating.

Forcing these hurting, terrified, and inflexible ewes to walk through Honey's ingenious footbath was the most disordered and upsetting battle I've ever been a part of. It was a clashing combat between the "stubborn ewes" versus us, the "stubborn twos." The ewes were bleating at us, we were bleating at them, and as I recall, we were bleating at each other.

When the mind-grinding grapple was over, we released the treated ewes into a new pasture. Then we continued with the overwhelming cleanup while dealing with the self-bashing trio singing in our ears, "I should have," "I could have," and "I'll never do that again!"

Our ewes responded quickly to the penicillin-streptomycin and their nightmarish footbath, and they were walking normally in a few days. We were sure they responded so quickly because they and their surroundings had been in such good condition. Thankfully, the infection would die out in the soil within fourteen days. But we knew we would have to be checking our sheep often, fastidiously keeping their feet trimmed for the next two years . . . foot rot can live in the hoof that long!

Early the next morning, Honey and I pitchforked the contaminated bedding out from the barn and dumped it into the center of the also-desecrated sheep paddock. We worked all day. It didn't feel like forward work, which is so rewarding, but rearward work. We were regrettably regressing.

When the girls came home from school, they joined us in removing the last stinking remains of the befouled bedding. Then, finally, the payoff came. We set the huge pile of contagion on fire. We felt compensated as this foul infection was finally annihilated.

> He [Jesus] will baptize us with the Holy Spirit and with fire. His winnowing fork is in his hand, and he will clear his threshing floor, gathering his wheat into the barn and burning up the chaff with unquenchable fire. (Matthew 3:11b–12)

Good Grain

The main reason our Shepherd appeared on earth was to destroy the devil's rotting contamination! (*Read 1 John 3:8 and Revelation 10:10*)

> All Scripture is God-breathed and is useful for teaching, rebuking, correcting, and training in righteousness, so that the man of God may be thoroughly equipped for every good work. (2 Timothy 3:16–17)

Our ewes responded quickly to the penicillin-streptomycin and their nightmarish footbath, and they were walking normally in a few days. We were sure they responded so quickly because they and their surroundings had been in such good condition. Thankfully the infection would die out in the soil within fourteen days. But we knew we would have to be checking our sheep often; fastidiously keeping their feet trimmed for the next two years . . . foot rot can live in the hoof that long!

Preach the Word; be prepared in season and out of season; correct, rebuke and encourage—with great patience and careful instruction. (2 Timothy 4:2)

The Shearing Shed

If you are in the process of eliminating a certain sin in your life, make sure you are in a church that preaches the Word of God. Humble yourself so you can accept correction and godly counsel. Join a small group or meet with one other person to whom you are accountable for a minimum of two years.

The abandoned sheep stalls, shed, paddock, and pastures colored our farm and our hearts a dismal gray. We missed seeing our ewes in and around the barn and up and down the hills. When the long and lonely two weeks were over, the whole family came out to the barn and the sheep shed to put down the classic golden pure-straw bedding that said to our ewes, "Welcome home!"

I have swept away your offenses like a cloud, your sins like the morning mist. Return to me, for I have redeemed you. (Isaiah 44:22)

Chew on This

When you feel the fire burning in your life, rejoice! Your Shepherd may be annihilating those areas contaminated by foot rot!

chapter seventeen

EVERY CLOUD
HAS A SILVER LINING

The whole family caught a nasty flu bug early in the winter, and it didn't leave until spring. I think we kept passing it back and forth. Several of us ended up with bronchitis and strep throat just as the lambing season started. Our doctor was afraid if we spent too much time in the barn, we'd end up with pneumonia. We lost a lot of lambs that season because we weren't able to be consistent with our barn checks.

I made it out to the barn to see Royal birth a boy and a girl lamb. They were both large, like their mother, and healthy looking. I wasn't expecting any problems with Royal or her babies because she had always been reliable and handled lambing well.

Two days later I was surprised to see her ewe lamb hunched over and shaky. I was thankful I dragged myself out to the barn, or she would have been gone by morning. After checking the situation, I discovered one of Royal's teats was infected, and she was only allowing the ram lamb to nurse on the healthy one.

I quickly picked up the girl and held her tight under my chin as I always did, and then I realized I couldn't smell her sweet baby lamb smell because my nose was so plugged.

"Now what should I do with you?" I asked the lamb.

I knew I didn't have any colostrum collected to give her, and I didn't have any lamb's milk left, and worse, I couldn't think. My head hurt so bad, all I wanted to do was jump back in bed. I gave Royal an injection for her obvious mastitis and held her while putting the lamb up to her good teat and discovered she was able to nurse. She nursed so hard and long she must have been starving.

Royal had made the decision to keep the boy and let her little girl die. Of course, both could have nursed off the same teat. But I knew only too well that when a ewe says no, she will never change her mind, even if the circumstances change. Had Royal been miraculously healed of her mastitis, she still wouldn't have taken her little girl back.

The Shearing Shed

Have we made judgments and decisions based on past circumstances or beliefs and are refusing to look at the situation in light of the present facts? Are we, like sheep, too stubborn and prideful to change? It's a sign of wisdom and strength to humble ourselves and say, "I've been wrong, and I've changed my mind."

I made a small pen for Royal and the lamb she accepted by cornering off a section of the larger lambing pen with portable three-board fences. The larger pen was filled with twelve of my best registered Suffolk ewes and their twenty-three black lambs. Suffolk lambs are born all black, and as they mature, their wool whitens while their heads and legs remain black.

I decided I would bring the rejected ewe lamb out with me to the barn every time I gave Royal her penicillin shot and let her nurse with her mom.

I pushed Royal against the fence and held her tight with my body while giving her the first shot. Then I deposited the baby up to her teat, slid a bale of straw up to them as close as I could, and dropped my two-hundred-pound stuffed head on the bale of straw . . . and miserably rested. I had to hold my left arm up, pressing firmly on Royal's shoulder, to keep her from bolting. It was the knifelike pain in that arm that ruined my rest.

In between feedings, I took the baby lamb into the house and plopped her down with whoever was dying on the nearest couch, loveseat, or La-Z-Boy. We named this little girl Baby—not intentionally; we were just too sick to give her a real name.

I was barely aware of a little head resting on the low fence board from the other side of the stall. It wasn't until my third or fourth visit of giving shots and letting the baby nurse that the suppressed vision caught up with me: this little black lamb has been watching me.

> I lift up my eyes to you, to you whose throne is in heaven. (Psalm 123:1)

I was astounded and delighted. His little face, upturned just a bit, had the most open and vulnerable expression I'd ever seen in a lamb. He was a picture of innocence and beauty.

This was my first relationship with a content, "need-nothing" lamb. I named this little guy after John, the beloved disciple who felt so loved by Jesus. Little John became one of my kids. I adopted him even though he had a wonderful birth mother.

He was a single lamb born to Judy, a highly bred, registered Suffolk ewe we purchased at the Michigan State University Ewe Sale the fall before. Judy was a wonderful mother, giving Little John all the milk and attention a lamb could ever want. In fact, he had enough milk for two. He had no apparent needs . . . yet he drew near. He was an inspiration to me, and I wanted to be like him.

They will see his face, and his name will be on their foreheads. (Revelation 22:4)

Little John was always there, waiting for me, wanting nothing. He so captured my heart that despite my fever and body aches, I reciprocated his presence and took him with me on my rounds. I let him cuddle with Baby and the girls in the house a few times, and he was rocked by Honey one night in front of the fire. We could love him because he would let us. What a treat he was.

Little John's response to me was not initiated by a calamity in his life or his desire to be fed. He simply chose to get to know me. He positioned his head on the bottom fence board and made himself available. I could do whatever I wanted to do with him. He trusted in me without really knowing me as well as our orphans did. Little John became my favorite lamb in all of Sheep World! He was truly a shining light in the unconscious populace of Sheep World.

Chew on This

Those who look to him are radiant; their faces are never covered with shame. (Psalm 34:5)

I introduced Little John to all the children, parents, and teachers who toured our farm that May, while telling his simple story. The message is so simple, calculating academic intellectuals could miss it.

Good Grain

Every day, position your head on the low fence board, tilt your head up just a bit, and rest in the Shepherd's presence and wait . . . just be there . . . available. Be open and expectant. Let Jesus love you; receive . . . receive.

Be prepared. He might speak to you or take you on his rounds; or his Father might whisk you up and comfort you right on his throne before the fire; you never know. I do know you will totally capture his heart. And remember, everyone who allows the Lord to love him is his favorite one!

Let us fix our eyes on Jesus, the author and perfecter of our faith. (Hebrews 12:2)

One thing have I asked of the Lord, that will I seek, inquire for and [insistently] require: that I may dwell in the house of the Lord [in His presence] all the days of my life, to behold and gaze upon the beauty [the sweet attractiveness and the delightful loveliness] of the Lord and to mediate, consider, and inquire in His temple. (Psalm 27:4 AMP) (Also read Psalm 16:11; 18:6; 65:4; and Luke 12:37)

chapter eighteen

THE SWEATER

"Honey, wouldn't it be nice to have something other than meat sheep grazing our pastures? Then we could keep the lambs. What do you think about us getting some wool sheep? We could sell their wool to spinners or take it to the Frankenmuth Woolen Mill. They sell producer's wool for quite a price."

It wasn't long before Honey located a sheep farmer wanting to sell one of his colored wool sheep. We piled the kids in the car and off we went. One of our youngest daughters, overhearing my positive conversation commented, "Are we gonna be rich?"

Her fleece was very long, of colors varying from black to shades of brown, blonde, and gray. She was a real beauty.

"It's about finding the right spinner," the owner said, "People will pay good money to get their hands on this quality of wool."

Jumping up and down, our daughter proclaimed, "I knew it! I knew it! We're gonna be rich!"

My honey loaded the ewe in the trailer, and we headed home with visions of sugar plums dancing in our heads.

"Honey, do you remember the name of her breed?"

"Kara-something, I think."

We had never heard of the name before. Finding out about this breed was put on my long list of things to do the next day.

When I first saw the ewe with her beautiful, long, wavy wool, I immediately thought of Marilyn, a foster daughter who lived with us for three years. She had beautiful, long, black, wavy hair that matched her vivacious personality. With determined resolution, I declared to the family, "This beautiful new ewe shall be named 'Marilyn.'"

Everyone looked at me, slightly puzzled, as I was breaking the rules of our naming game. We were supposed to decide on a name together, and it wasn't supposed to be a friend or a relative. They obviously could tell I wasn't asking them but telling them, so Marilyn it was.

Flushing season sneaked up on me, and before I knew it, it was too late to find out about Marilyn's breed and locate a similar ram. She would have to be bred with our Suffolk, Abraham. I was mad at myself for letting this happen.

"We'll start our lucrative wool business next year, Honey, when I have more time. This year we'll find out what kind of mother she is." I must be positive . . .

Five months later, Marilyn had twins. She delivered them alone in the night. They were beautiful twin ewes with shiny, black, tight, curly wool. They were licked dry and nursing strong when we found them. There wasn't a trace of afterbirth in the pen, and everything was in order.

"It looks like we've got a winner!"

I asked my mother if she would like to knit a sweater from Marilyn's wool. My mom loved the idea and shared my enthusiasm for such a priceless keepsake for the family. I asked the shearers to set Marilyn's fleece aside for me on shearing day, and I took her wool to the woolen mill in Frankenmuth, where it was washed, carded, and spun for knitting.

As soon as my mom received the hand-spun yarn, she started her exciting project. She had been knitting the special wool for several days when I received a phone call.

"I just thought you'd like to know, I'm going to have to lay the knitting down for a while because my hands are getting sore."

I wondered if my mom might be getting a little arthritis. A few days later she called again.

"Are you sure this is Marilyn's wool? It's so heavy and thick; now my arms and neck are hurting."

I assured her it was Marilyn's wool and suggested she take some ibuprofen.

"Maybe you should stop by and take another look at this wool," she told me.

"It's so thick the mill couldn't even get all the straw out."

Sure enough, the new sweater had bits and pieces of yellow straw intertwined in the heavy yarns. I immediately got in touch with the previous owner and asked him the name of Marilyn's breed. He told me she was a Karakul sheep and assured me it was excellent wool. Again, I went to the library.

The Karakul sheep produce very coarse wool. It is classified as "carpet wool." They produce wool for tweed, carpets, and mattresses. My poor mother was knitting a mattress!

With pure determination, Mom finished the carpet cardigan, but the weight and warmth of it was unbearable. I was thankful my poor mom's hands, arms, and neck healed—and her fingernails grew back—but I felt terrible. It was entirely my fault.

In my study of the Karakul sheep, I also discovered their lambs are used to make fur coats . . . the very expensive, sought-after Persian lamb fur coats. The lambs are killed when they are three to ten days old, before their curl straightens. Did I ask the Lord before I started this project? I think not. Did I find out the gifts this particular sheep could bring to my flock? No, I didn't. And because I used the wrong sheep for the job, my poor mother endured days of pain and wasted her valuable time.

> Just as each of us has one body with many members, and these members do not all have the same function, so in Christ we who are many form one body, and each member belongs to all the others. We have different gifts, according to the grace given us. (Romans 12:4–6a)

The Shearing Shed

It is wrong for shepherds to use accommodating sheep to accomplish their own goals. It is imperative that the shepherd find out the unique call God has given each one of his sheep. Encourage those sheep to gather regularly for prayer and fellowship with other sheep who have the same call. Then watch God work! These sheep will go out and do the works that Jesus did!

Chew on This

Do you feel like you're knitting a mattress? If so, you're probably not doing what God intended for your life. God has a unique plan and purpose for each one of us, wherein we use our unique set of gifts, talents, strengths, and weaknesses. In his plan, our knitting will produce soft and luxurious sweaters!

chapter nineteen

HOLY AND PERFECT

Marilyn was with us longer than any other ewe. Eventually we realized that Marilyn was special. She had never caused us one problem. Even her hooves grew at a slow pace, hardly ever needing trimming. She was what horse-boarding-people call "an easy-keeper."

Whenever our dog sneaked in through the gate to the sheep pasture, the ewes would become hysterical and run helter-skelter in a million directions. Their frenzy temporarily deleted their memories, and their lambs were on their own—except for Marilyn's. Marilyn would nuzzle her twins to move in really close, almost under her, and defiantly stand her ground and pound her hooves at our Christy. She stood her ground in the face of the enemy! She was fearless.

When our lambs were about two or three months old, their mothers would allow them to come together without them for short periods of play. They usually played "the wave," named by our kids, of course. All the lambs joined in the game except Marilyn's kids. Instead, she would take her lambs to the far side of the pasture to graze with her.

Very rarely have I seen a ewe with lambs isolate herself from the rest of the flock. I'd like to think Marilyn took her lambs away so they couldn't watch the other lambs having so much fun. But the truth was, Marilyn felt the danger of the game was worse than the danger of being isolated. After a few weeks, when nothing bad happened, Marilyn would allow her lambs to join the others. Periodically she would call them to her right in the middle of the game, and they would hightail it to her so fast Honey and I could only drool.

"Now, there's a picture of respect and obedience! Why can't our kids mind us that fast?" we would say.

Sometimes Marilyn would let her lambs go right back to the game. We think she was testing their obedience.

> He must manage his own family well and see that his children obey him with proper respect. (If anyone does not know how to manage his own family, how can he take care of God's church?) (1 Timothy 3:4–5)

We realized Marilyn never once needed our assistance when she delivered. That's because we never saw her deliver. Every year she gave birth to nine-pound black twins in the middle of the night when no one was around. We would find her in the morning, lying in the straw, with her twins sleeping tight against her warm, woolly body, dry and clean, with rounded tummies. The lambing pen was always as spotless and unruffled as they were. Someone would always say, "No help needed here."

Marilyn was calm for her vaccinations, shearing, trimming, and even at feeding time. And that says a lot. Sheep gobble their grain and often jump right into the feeder, landing on top of another ewe or even their own lambs. They seem to lose their dignity when they see food. They devour, gulp, and regurgitate . . . but not Marilyn. I thought maybe she was timid, as she was always the last one to start eating. As we talked about her qualities, we realized there was nothing timid about Marilyn. Could sheep have good manners? I often slipped her extra grain when the other ewes weren't looking.

> Give her the reward she has earned, and let her works bring her praise at the city gate. (Proverbs 31:31)

The only thing we didn't especially care for about Marilyn was the fact that she didn't have a tail, but Karakul sheep don't have tails. In place of a tail is a wide layer of fat, a slight hump, notice-able right after shearing. By the karakul standard, Marilyn was 100 percent.

We were in complete agreement: Marilyn exemplified mother-hood in Sheep World. She stood out as a composite portrait of the ideal ewe! She reminded us of the woman in Proverbs 31 for the way she garnered our respect and admiration. Was she perfect? Pretty close. She would remind us to do all things with excellence and to answer the high call of holiness.

Marilyn persevered in her exemplary mothering until her death from old age.

> Perseverance must finish its work so that you may be mature and complete, not lacking anything. (James 1:4)

> Her children praise her, and with great pride her husband says, There are many good women, but you are the best! Charm can be deceiving, and beauty fades away, but a woman who honors the Lord deserves to be praised. Show her respect—praise her in public for what she has done. (Proverbs 31:28–31 cev)

We who are the sheep of God's pasture must live out the spiri-tual standards Jesus gave us in Matthew 5, 6, and 7. If we do, we will find ourselves walking through life on the "Highway of Holiness," or as it is sometimes called, "the Way of Holiness," with Jesus our Shepherd in the lead. Remember, only those who have received salvation by faith in Jesus Christ are traveling on this highway. These spiritual standards are opposite what the world has set up. The world's standards ultimately lead to our destruction, while the standards Jesus gives us lead to life. The call to perfec-tion or holiness is the high call to seek God above all else, with all of our heart, soul, mind, and emotions, and to love our neighbor as ourself.

If you love those who love you, what reward will you get? Are not even the tax collectors doing that? And if you greet only your brothers, what are you doing more than others? Do not even pagans do that? Be perfect, therefore, as your heavenly Father is perfect. (Matthew 5:46-48)

"Through Christ's death and resurrection, once and for all, He made His believers perfect in God's sight. At the same time, He is making them holy as they follow and obey Him. He is progressively cleansing and setting us apart for His special use in our daily lives. We should not be surprised, ashamed or shocked that we still need to grow. God is not finished with us yet. We can encourage this growth process by deliberately applying Scripture to all areas of our lives, by accepting the discipline and guidance Christ provides, and by giving Him control of our desires and goals. (*Life Application Study Bible* NIV, commentary on Hebrews 10:14)

Chew on This

To be holy and perfect is to be possessed of God. Our loving deeds don't perfect us; rather, as God perfects us, we'll do loving deeds for him. Read Philippians 3:1-15.

Good Grain

Through Christ's death and resurrection, once and for all, he made his believers perfect in God's sight. At the same time, he is making them holy as they follow and obey him. . . because by one sacrifice he has made perfect forever those who are being made holy. (Hebrews 10:14) *chapter twenty*

THE LUKEWARM

Because sheep do not understand soil conservation techniques, they will graze in one area until it is bare. Their view of life is limited to the little patch of grass that is under their noses. They are a danger to the environment because they don't care about anything but what they can get for themselves. Sound familiar? They'll eat until they're licking dirt.

Honey fenced off our largest sheep pasture into four smaller sections, and every week I would put the ewes in a new section. To get to the new section of pasture, I had to lead the sheep through a long and narrow lane at the end of the cow pasture. This lane was equipped with Honey's high-powered electric fence. This Australian fence system was designed to get the electric current through the sheep's dense wool. Our sheep learned to walk single file in one day! Walking down that lane would bring back memories of my years in a private school, walking single file, in silence, lined up according to height, and a ruler snapping if we got out of line. The sheep's fast pace required me to walk very briskly, or the ewe behind me would step on my heels. I considered this my best ewe-aerobic exercise.

One morning as the ewes and I arrived at the gate to the new pasture, I didn't move aside fast enough and the ewes knocked me down and ran right over me to get to the grass. Of course, I rolled over and out of the way quickly and only endured a few painful sheep feet. My feelings were more injured than my body. I was saddened. I realized with a deeper comprehension that day just how pitiful, wretched, poor, and blind my sheep were. After all the years of shepherding them, except for my orphans, our relationship was still lukewarm or nonexistent. Like Jesus, I was ready to spit them out of my mouth! Almost simultaneously I saw myself and the larger body of believers also pitiful, wretched, poor, blind, and naked. I was heartsick.

I know your deeds, that you are neither cold nor hot. I wish you were either one or the other! So, because you are lukewarm—neither hot nor cold—I am about to spit you out of my mouth. You say, I am rich; I have acquired wealth and do not need a thing. But you do not realize that you are wretched, pitiful, poor, blind and naked." (Revelation 3:15–17)

The Shearing Shed

Lord, I don't want to be like my self-consumed sheep, running right over you and breaking your heart. I want to run to you and please you above all else. Take away my sheep's heart and give me a heart on fire for you.

I counsel you to buy from me gold refined in the fire, so you can become rich; and white clothes to wear, so you can cover your shameful nakedness; and salve to put on your eyes, so you can see. (Revelation 3:18)

I always enjoyed the weekly ritual of bringing the ewes to their new pasture. Whenever time and weather permitted, I took that time to sit in the clean grass, with the sheep munching all around me, to be with my Shepherd. I considered the sheep pastures to be some of my "secret places" where I prayed alone with God. I especially loved meeting the Lord on the fourth pasture, which was the highest spot on our property. It was adorned with a few vintage apple trees providing shade and an overview of the land that reminded me of the saints in heaven looking down on us, urging us on.

Here's what I want you to do: Find a quiet, secluded place so you won't be tempted to role-play before God. Just be there as simply and honestly as you can manage. The focus will shift from you to God, and you will begin to sense his grace. (Matthew 6:6 MSG)

One early summer day, as I prayed in the high pasture, the Spirit of the Lord touched me in a unique way. In one instant I went from looking around the pasture to watching a big-screen panorama on an IMAX screen. There on the screen were four shivering orphan lambs braving an intense rainstorm with menacing thunder and lightning piercing the black sky over them. In the distance I could see another group of lambs nursing with their mothers and frolicking in the warm and lighted barn.

I looked back at the orphan lambs, and now they appeared as disciplined and alert soldiers—focused only on my coming. At first I assumed they were miserable, that is until I looked into their eyes. Their eyes were brilliantly glowing with the glory of God! As I continued to look, I felt the drawing power of God moving me toward them. It was as though I were on a high-speed airport escalator, heading straight for them and the magnificent light in their eyes. They saw me coming toward them, and all four lambs leaped up in the air and bounced and bleated with such love that I thought my heart was being drawn right out of my body. They truly captured my heart! In one instant they were mine and I was theirs! What an interchange! We were one.

I have given them the glory that you gave me, that they may be one as we are one: I in them and you in me. (John 17:22–23)

Righteous Father, though the world does not know you, I know you, and they know that you have sent me. I have made you known to them, and will continue to make you known in order that the love you have for me may be in them and that I myself may be in them. (John 17:25–26) (Also read 1 Thessalonians 3:12–13 in the *Amplified Bible.*)

Whenever I thought about those vigilant orphans waiting for me, I would remember Jesus telling us that he would leave our world but would return one day. He gave us a warning—to keep watch for his return.

"It will be good for those servants whose master finds them watching when he comes . . . You also must be ready, because the Son of Man will come at an hour when you do not expect him." (Luke 12:37, 40)

Honey would give a similar message to our kids whenever we left for the day or for an evening out:

"Now, you kids be good. Do your chores, and no fighting. Keep the house clean, don't let anyone in, and have a good time."

"Yeah, right. Dad. When will you and Mom be back?"

And with a deep voice he would slowly reply, "When you least expect it."

"No one knows about that day or hour, not even the angels in heaven, nor the Son, but only the Father . . . Therefore keep watch, because you do not know on what day your Lord will come . . . So you also must be ready, because the Son of Man will come at an hour when you do not expect him." (Matthew 24:36, 42, 44)

Good Grain

The orphaned bummers are the blessed ones! Only a broken and hungry sheep will draw in the presence of God.

Chew on This

Satisfied, complacent sheep are indifferent and separated from God. God has given man the freedom to choose whom he will follow, and God will never override his will. Without God, Satan is free to work indifference, separation, and division in man's life. With God, man is on the path of love, unity and oneness.

The Shearing Shed

Are you hungry for God? Are you willing to let him do whatever it takes to get you to that place of broken, holy hunger? Are you willing to give the Shepherd total control over your life? If you do, don't be shocked if he starts messing with it. He might put you in a new pasture, in a different sheep pen, or even lock you up in a smelly stall for awhile; whatever it takes. Don't hold on to any part of your life so tight that the Shepherd can't move it around or eliminate it! He alone knows your future. You have to believe that the plans he has for you are always for your good . . . even if they stink for a time.

"For I know the plans I have for you," declares the LORD, "plans to prosper you and not to harm you, plans to give you hope and a future." (Jeremiah 29:11)

chapter twenty-one

THE GATES OF PRAISE

It was an unusually sunny fall morning after a month of rain. The pastures were once again lush and bright green, looking more like spring than fall. Every animal in residence had been getting a shower every day, and now they were so clean they sparkled.

From where I was standing I could see the horse, cow, and sheep pastures all at once. The respective animals were all spread out and able to graze without competition. Our two fearless geese were running at top speed from one pasture to another, squawking at everything that moved, sending up birds of every color. Both spring-born mares were lying in the grass, sunbathing, while their mothers grazed nearby. Then the sunlight hit the brass ring attached to the nose of our bull, Intimidation. I didn't realize he had grown so much; he had finally grown into his name. I was overcome with God's created beauty.

> You water all [the] fields and level the lumpy ground. You send showers of rain to soften the soil and help the plants sprout . . . Meadows are filled with sheep and goats; valleys overflow with grain and echo with joyful songs. (Psalm 65:10, 13 CEV)

I actually thought I heard the towering white pines singing praise to their Creator that morning.

> Let the fields be jubilant, and everything in them. Then all the trees of the forest will sing for joy. (Psalm 96:12)

The day's first load of wash would have to wait—it was just too beautiful out in paradise. I decided to walk to the back sheep pasture and check on the sheep. I wanted to prolong this fullness of gratitude that seemed about ready to burst from my heart. I entered the pasture; Jellybean greeted me, and several of the "lukewarm" sheep actually looked up. I was starting to overflow. Then I did the most incredible thing: I began singing and dancing in and around my sheep. I was singing a beautiful love song I'd never heard before. It just flowed out of me, and I didn't mince on the volume either. I really bellowed it out. It was a song of gratitude and praise to the Lord of this earth.

> Sing to the LORD a new song; sing to the LORD, all the earth. Sing to the LORD, praise his name; proclaim his salvation day after day. (Psalm 96:1–2)

I have never danced like I did that morning. I felt weightless. I even grabbed Jellybean and spun him around with me a few times. When I put Jellybean down, he stumbled on his feet for a bit; he was dizzy. I laughed . . . we were dancing!

> Let them praise his name with dancing and make music to him with tambourine and harp. For the LORD takes delight in his people. (Psalm 149:3–5)

The next thing I knew, I was twirling around a few of the lukewarm lambs one by one. I was no longer focused on the Lord but on them. I was filled with an incredible love for each one of them, but I knew it wasn't for them but for us, God's people. I was experiencing a touch of God's incredible love for us! He's crazy about us! I danced and sang and danced for an unknown period of time. I was both a participant and a witness.

The LORD your God is with you, he is mighty to save. He will take great delight in you, he will quiet you with his love, he will rejoice over you with singing. (Zephaniah 3:17)

Suddenly the flow stopped. I looked around . . . the atmosphere was different. I could see flies and thistles in the pasture. The sheep really needed shearing, and I noticed the rain had eroded one side of the hill. What happened? My vision was altered. I was no longer seeing with spiritual eyes.

The immense love that had so filled me was now replaced with an uncomfortable self-consciousness. I had been singing and dancing with sheep! I automatically searched the perimeters for onlookers. Why, I don't know. There was only one border of our property visible from where I stood, and I had never seen anyone there before. Unbelievably, my deepest fear materialized. I spotted a man in the corner, up in a tree! Instantly my face flushed, beginning warm, ending fire-hot. I was embarrassed. I didn't want him to know I saw him, and I started humming, like everything was cool. I took one more look, making sure it wasn't an illusion. Yup, he was still there . . . just staring. I quickly exited the stage, certain there was a pie dripping down my face.

I sprinted to the house and called Honey at work. I told him I saw a man up in a tree, right at the corner of our property. "I was singing and dancing with the sheep . . . and he saw me."

Honey didn't ask any questions about my performance, as though I danced regularly. He just matter-of-factly told me that it was bow-hunting season, and the guy was just looking for deer, and to stay out of that area. Then he asked me, "What did the guy look like?"

"I'm not sure, but I bet his mouth hung open."

This is love; not that we loved God, but that he loved us and sent his Son as an atoning sacrifice for our sins. (1 John 4:10)

The love I experienced that morning changed my life. I knew I would never be content to spend the rest of my life focused on my patch of grass, no matter how comfortable it was. I wanted more of the God that created us. He made us. We belong to him. We are his people, the sheep of his pasture.

The Good Shepherd brought me to a verdant pasture that day. I had a taste of spiritual food that fed me like no amount of earthly food could ever do. I now understood how to get into his awesome pasture: all I had to do was go through his gate singing praises, giving thanks, and adoring him!

The Shearing Shed

Apart from God I was a prideful and self-centered sheep. I realized I was more concerned about what that stranger thought about me than what God thought about me. Then I realized again . . . it isn't about me, it's all about him. He's the lover and I'm the loved sheep. He loves me because he is so filled with love . . . he is love!

Good Grain

On your feet now—applaud GOD! Bring a gift of laughter, sing yourselves into his presence. Know this: GOD is God, and God, GOD. He made us; we didn't make him. We're his people, his well-tended sheep. Enter with the password: "Thank you!" Make yourselves at home, talking praise. Thank him. Worship him. For GOD is sheer beauty, all-generous in love, loyal always and ever. (Psalm 100 MSG)

chapter twenty-two

SERVANT LOVE

One of the exercises listed in my ewe-aerobics program was "crotching" the sheep. I can still hear the comments from my daughters, "Mother, that's gross! What a horrible, nasty name!"

"Are you really going to do it? 'Crotch' the sheep?"

They laughed while emphasizing the name. Years later I found out my daughters thought I had made up that offensive name. I didn't. Crotching was listed and described in all my magazines along with all the other highfalutin things a shepherd does for his sheep.

If the sheep are not sheared before lambing, the shepherd must cut away the manure-coated tags of wool surrounding the udder and scrub the area clean. Unless this is done, the lamb loss would be extremely high due to starvation or infection.

Jane, my assistant shepherd, volunteered to help me do this terribly unpleasant job every year. We were always laughing and muttering indignant comments such as, "Do you believe we're really doing this?"

"Mom, this is gross."

"If our friends could see us now."

We realized it was one of the most unpleasant jobs on the farm. But strangely, this simple, unpleasant job, if bypassed, could lead to the deaths of many of our lambs. It had to be done.

My memory of actually crotching the ewes takes me back to a numbingly cold barn about a week or two before lambing. The barn would be bleak, depressing, and lifeless. The pregnant ewes were expressionless and so full of babies they could hardly move. They would just stand and stare, motionless except for the chewing of their cud. Of course they couldn't move. Not only were they full of babies but their wool coats carried on and in them a whole year's worth of earthy matter!

Jane and I would carefully bring the expectant mothers down on the floor of the barn, one by one. They were especially frightened because they knew they could never get up on their own. In fact, if a ewe stays on her back for too long, she will suffocate. We talked to them in low, calming tones to quell their rising anxiety. We gently touched the moving babies in their bellies—one or two on each side, resting on the floor.

"Jane, do you think this one has triplets? Could it be quads? Look, this one is kicking."

We carefully clipped off the foul-smelling tags of wool while trying to breathe normally. We were actually happy when the barn was glacially cold because the warmer the temperature, the worse the smell.

We continued to calm the frightened ewes with our soothing intonations as we washed their malodorous udders and the surrounding area with warm, soapy water. We applied ointment on every wound, boil, or area of chafing. Then with much satisfaction, we released our heavily pregnant mothers with their squeaky-clean undersides to their "waiting rooms." We would leave the barn, smiling as visions of itty-bitty lambs danced in our heads.

The sensible solution to eliminate crotching the sheep every year was simple—get them sheared before lambing season. I contacted a reputable shearing company from Traverse City, Michigan, hoping I could get our farm on their itinerary late January or early in February. They informed me that they didn't work with small sheep farms because it would take them longer to set up their equipment than it would to shear the flock. They suggested we bring our sheep to the nearest large farm in the area, and they would shear them there. Happily, the largest sheep operation in our area was Milo's farm. I contacted our wonderful neighbor, and he agreed and gave us his shearing date—in late April, after lambing season.

It took Honey an hour to get our frightened sheep loaded in the trailer and about three minutes to drive to Milo's place. We arrived early in the afternoon, just in case they finished shearing Milo's flocks ahead of schedule, and then we waited . . . and waited. For some reason, they misjudged their timeline and didn't finish until early evening. The shearers told us that they were very sorry, but their shearers were exhausted and finished for the day. The man in charge had sympathy for our situation and surprisingly agreed to drive the few miles to our farm the next morning on their way out of the area.

The next morning, the most gigantic moving van you ever saw pulled into our driveway to the barn. Our gravel driveway compressed several inches, and I felt the weight of the truck move across the yard. They parked next to the barn, making it look small-scale. These shearers were capable of shearing thousands of sheep per job. They had been camped at Milo's place for three days.

They were right. It did take them longer to set up their equipment than it did to shear our little flock. And as incredible as it sounds, the man in charge offered to come to our place every year after finishing at Milo's place. We were astonished by his generous offer, and we thanked our Good Shepherd for this unanticipated gift.

Yet, year after year, the shearers were scheduled to come to our place in late spring. I couldn't schedule our lambing season that late because of the flies and other pesky insects. I had no choice. I was to crotch the ewes before lambing season all the sixteen years I raised sheep. I was to be personally impacted in spirit and through all my senses with the servant message. I figured it must be important.

> Sitting down, Jesus called the Twelve and said, "If anyone wants to be first, he must be the very last, and the servant of all." (Mark 9:35)

I often wondered, if I had a large sheep operation, would I give this smelly, backbreaking job to the hired help? Possibly.

Then I remembered Jesus, kneeling down at the feet of each disciple. I could envision him dipping a cloth in a basin of warm water, just as Jane and I had done, and lovingly washing the feet of his disciples. Jesus and his disciples walked along the same paths as the sheep did, so I'm sure he washed off the same gross and smelly materials we did! Jesus wanted us to know that he did not come to be served, but to serve, and we were to do likewise.

> Now that I, your Lord and Teacher, have washed your feet, you also should wash one another's feet. (John 13:14)

Chew on This

I thought about shepherds of churches that have designated all the dirty work to others. I began to see the grave temptation of losing one's servant heart, perhaps thinking we are too important or too busy to be bothered with serving others.

"You've observed how godless rulers throw their weight around," he said, "and when people get a little power how quickly it goes to their heads. It's not going to be that way with you. Whoever wants to be great must become a servant. Whoever wants to be first among you must be your slave. That is what the Son of Man has done: He came to serve, not to be served—and then to give away his life in exchange for many who are held hostage." (Mark 10:42–45 MSG)

Good Grain

Our leadership and authority must be the result of our relationship to Jesus Christ and our daily imitation of him. We are to be like him—a servant-leader.

chapter twenty-three

JELLYBEAN, THE EVANGELIST

That which was from the beginning, which we have heard, which we have seen with our eyes, which we have looked at and our hands have touched—this we proclaim concerning the Word of life. The life appeared; we have seen it and testify to it, and we proclaim to you the eternal life, which was with the Father and has appeared to us. We proclaim to you what we have seen and heard, so that you also may have fellowship with us. And our fellowship is with the Father and with his Son, Jesus Christ. (1 John 1:1–4)

The Greek word for evangel is *euangelion,* which means "good news" or "gospel." *Euangelos* means "bringing good news" and "the messenger." *Evangelism* means "the winning or revival of personal commitments to Christ."

Webster's definition of an evangelist is "a writer or preacher of the good news." My definition of an evangelist is "Jellybean," and I believe we are all called to be Jellybeans.

Jellybean was born in April 1987. He was a registered Suffolk ram. I did not record the unfortunate circumstances that led to his adoption under the name of "Jellybean." I did record that he had pneumonia, likely caused from milk getting in his lungs the first week of his life. I had written in the corner "not good." I administered 3cc of penicillin twice a day for one week, 1cc of Banamin for fever, and 1cc of Genticin, specifically for pneumonia in animals.

We knew how dangerous bottle-feeding newborn lambs could be. If the hungry lamb nursed too hard or the hole in the nipple was too large, the lamb would end up choking and inhaling the milk, and that was usually fatal.

There is an old saying with shepherds, "A sick sheep is a dead sheep." Why? Bringing in a veterinarian costs more than the price of the average sheep. If the common antibiotic given doesn't do the trick, the shepherd may have to let the sheep go for financial reasons.

Our veterinarian once told us that the problem with sheep is they do not have hope. He explained that pain or sickness will so overwhelm a sheep that it will give up right away and die.

Chew on This

Man will also give up and die without hope. Hope is a gift of life given to mankind by God. With hope, man can anticipate, aspire, and believe in what he does not see. The Lord delights in those who can put their hope in him and his unfailing love.

Jellybean was born right after the Easter our whole family went black-jellybean-crazy. Everyone was trying to exchange red and green jellybeans for those really good black ones. I finally bought a bag of black jellybeans to add to everyone's diminishing Easter baskets. It was very easy to name this little black orphan that Easter. Though the sheep industry calls these orphaned lambs "bummers," I don't think Jellybean would have felt his plight was "a bummer."

Jane came down with mononucleosis just before lambing season and spent her Easter vacation on the love seat in front of the fireplace in the kitchen-and-dining area. Thus Jellybean had a full-time shepherd he could snuggle with. Normally, our orphan lambs only stayed in the house two or three days, but this little lamb was able to stay with Jane throughout her Easter vacation. Jane and Jellybean both recovered from their ailments.

The kitchen-dining-family area was the hub of the house. All interactions and activities either happened there or were instigated from this focal point. Therefore Jellybean saw and heard it all. He learned to acclimate himself to every family member and every guest. He played hard with Jimmy, and when the two of them were yelled at for getting too rowdy, he would run and jump into Jane's arms. Jane liberally fed him small amounts of milk from his bottle. He anticipated pats, hugs, and kisses from every person he encountered, and he put up with baths and diapers and became good friends with our dog. He was part of the family.

Jellybean's familiarity with us changed him. He wasn't like the other lambs that were always so afraid. He lost his fear of man and dog. He became very pliable and easily adapted to whatever we were doing. He was most content when he was with Jane. Sometimes he lay next to her, motionless, for hours at a time. And he no longer smelled like a sheep . . . he smelled like Jane. Jane and Jellybean wore Love's Baby Soft perfume.

But thanks be to God, who always leads us in triumphal procession in Christ and through us spreads everywhere the fragrance of the knowledge of him. For we are to God the aroma of Christ among those who are being saved and those who are perishing. To the one we are the smell of death; to the other, the fragrance of life. (2 Corinthians 2:14–16)

Good Grain

> If we spend enough time with the Good Shepherd, we will have his aroma.

We received a phone call from a pastor who heard we had an orphaned lamb in our house and wondered if he could borrow him for their upcoming Sunday service.

Early Sunday morning we had Jellybean all cleaned up, extra diaper in tow, and sent him on his first evangelistic mission. We sent him, not because he was gifted or special, but because he was the most familiar with his shepherd and he was available.

Jellybean went on four missions that Easter season. What message did he bring to the churches? Well, it wasn't about him! One youth pastor told me he brought Jellybean on stage in front of all the kids at children's church, and when he removed his diaper, Jellybean stood there, trembling, and tinkled . . . to the hilarious howling of the kids. No, it wasn't about him; he was just a sheep. His message wasn't about how much he knew or how well he could communicate. He didn't come with elegance. He simply came with the aroma of the master . . . all over him.

> When I came to you, brothers, I did not come with eloquence or superior wisdom as I proclaimed to you the testimony about God . . . I came to you in weakness and fear, and with much trembling. (1 Corinthians 2:1, 3)

If Jellybean could have gone back into Sheep World as an evangelist, I don't believe he would have given his fellow sheep a five-point sermon. He was the sermon. And if he did speak, it would have been quite simple. It would have been about the love he received from me, his shepherd, and how he was radically changed by that love . . . and it would have been about what he saw me do and what he heard me say.

> For we cannot help speaking about what we have seen and heard. (Acts 4:20)

> We proclaim to you what we have seen and heard, so that you also may have fellowship with us. And our fellowship is with the Father and with his Son, Jesus Christ. (1 John 1:3)

No, I don't think Jellybean could have kept his mouth shut. I think he would have had to tell his sheep buddies the good news about the shepherd and his family or he would have burst. His buddies would have listened to him, too, because their friend was no longer the same. He didn't even smell the same. And he even loved the master's dog—their enemy!

> When they saw the courage of Peter and John and realized that they were unschooled, ordinary men, they were astonished and they took note that these men had been with Jesus. (Acts 4:13)

> I tell you, whoever acknowledges me before men, the Son of Man will also acknowledge him before the angels of God. (Luke 12:8)

Maybe Jellybean would have said something like this: "Fellow sheep, look up! Your Shepherd is here. Yup, that's right, right here in our pasture. He's waiting patiently for you to look up and acknowledge his presence.

You say you can't see him? All you have to do is set aside your natural vision and ask him to help you to see and hear him with your spiritual eyes and ears. He's just waiting for you to ask. He's actually longing to communicate with you, but he'll never override you. He'll just wait until you long to communicate with him. It's about your "wanting" to know him. If you want enough, you will.

You still can't hear him? Have you acknowledged him? Have you told him you want him to be your Shepherd? If you do, oh . . . you'll experience the love he has had for you before you were ever born. His love for you is not just for this life either, but for all eternity!

This is what happens: when you decide to follow the Shepherd for the rest of your life, he'll give you his Spirit, and his Spirit is your guarantee that it will happen. It's his Spirit that will enable you to recognize him, to hear him speak to you, and to know mysteries from his house that are just too numerous to count. No one from Sheep World can know the thoughts of the Shepherd, unless they have his Spirit. And without his Spirit, they would think the things he has said and done were crazy and ridiculous; they wouldn't understand them at all. Why? They are only discerned spiritually.

> The man without the Spirit does not accept the things that come from the Spirit of God, for they are foolishness to him, and he cannot understand them, because they are spiritually discerned. (1 Corinthians 2:14)

> Jesus answered, "I tell you the truth, no one can enter the kingdom of God unless he is born of water and the Spirit. Flesh gives birth to flesh, but the Spirit gives birth to spirit." (John 3:5–6)

Did I tell you I've heard our Shepherd singing songs over us? Love songs. When I enter into his songfests, I get a whole new picture of how glorious, holy, and powerful he really is! His glory almost knocks me over! I think a smidgen of it is rubbing off on me. Have you noticed that I keep humming his songs, and I've started to do the things I've seen him do? Not all the time, but I've started. And my heart is different . . . I love everyone; even the grouchy old rams. Sheep World also looks different to me now. It was made just for us by our shepherd, you know. It's beautiful, with green meadows, nutritious food and clear running water all piped in for us. We really should stop polluting it. If we did, it would sure take a load off of him. He'd love it.

I also found out he understands our pain. He hurts so bad when we hurt, that if we comfort the hurting, he tells us, we are doing it to him! I also know that everything he does to us, he does for our good. We don't have to ask why; we just have to trust.

Fellow sheep, I realize this radical kind of love that the Shepherd has for us can be hard to swallow—its so un-sheep-like! You'll just have to experience it for yourself.

> So that Christ may dwell in your hearts through faith. And I pray that you, being rooted and established in love, may have power, together with all the saints, to grasp how wide and long and high and deep is the love of Christ, and to know this love that surpasses knowledge—that you maybe filled to the measure of all the fullness of God. (Ephesians 3:17–19)

Remember when those two stray dogs got into our pasture? And the time we all got foot rot and were banished from the barn for two weeks? Remember the summer there wasn't any rain and our pasture was burned to a crisp? That was terrible. You'll be glad to know that none of these things, and other things too horrible to mention, can separate us from his Love.

> Do you think anyone is going to be able to drive a wedge between us and Christ's love for us? There is no way! Not trouble, not hard times, not hatred, not hunger, not homelessness, not bullying threats, not backstabbing, not even the worst sins listed in Scripture . . . none of this fazes us because Jesus loves us. I'm absolutely convinced that nothing—nothing living or dead,

angelic or demonic, today or tomorrow, high or low, thinkable or unthinkable – absolutely nothing can get between us and God's love because of the way that Jesus our Master has embraced us. (Romans 8:35–39 MSG)

Everything I have seen and heard I have told you. I've told you, hoping that you would want to join me in living an entirely new kind of life—a spiritual life walking daily with our Shepherd. Please consider this offer seriously, my friends. Remember, I know for a fact, he loves each one of us beyond description.

My response is to get down on my knees before the Father, this magnificent Father who parcels out all heaven and earth. I ask him to strengthen you by his Spirit—not a brute strength but a glorious inner strength—that Christ will live in you as you open the door and invite him in. And I ask him that with both feet planted firmly on love, you'll be able to take in with all followers of Jesus the extravagant dimensions of Christ's love. Reach out and experience the breadth! Test its length! Plumb the depths! Rise to the heights! Live full lives, full in the fullness of God. (Ephesians 3:14–19 MSG)

chapter twenty-four

OUR IMPERISHABLE INHERITANCE

The Lord gave our family a miraculous sign that exemplified the wonderful hope of 1 Peter 1:4. I pray the following story will inspire you, the reader, to receive the hope that is offered to all of mankind. This story took place about a month before we left our beautiful home in suburbia for the farm.

I was beyond busy. I had a Supermom's schedule without the "super" abilities. I was in over my head and decided to consciously ask God to help me with every decision I had to make. I was packing up the house, enrolling the kids in their new schools, working with Honey on the blueprints for the addition, ordering kitchen cabinets, light fixtures, paint colors, plus all the things a mom does every day when she has six kids and two indoor dogs. Before I knew it, everything was marked off my list except for one thing: "pick out the carpeting." I was excited because after the carpet was installed, we could move in.

The minute I felt the soft, luxurious green carpet the store owner showed me, I knew my decision was made.

"But you haven't seen this carpet in blue. It's just as beautiful."

"This also comes in blue?" Oh, no . . . another decision. I told him I would call him with my decision within the week.

It was a decision I couldn't make, yet for some reason I didn't seek the Lord about it. I didn't trust him to guide my decision. Instead, I started asking everyone I knew, "What do you think: should we get green or blue carpet?"

In so many words, my family and everyone I asked all told me, "There isn't a right answer; it's whatever you want." But I didn't know what I wanted. I started asking our neighbors, ladies in the grocery store who smiled at me, the person sitting next to me in church, and one of the girls' new teachers. I was immersed in my miserable indecisiveness and drove everybody nuts.

A woman with a beautiful smile, named Mary, came to help me with the cleaning. Of course, I asked Mary her opinion about the carpet . . . all throughout the day. I was getting good at presenting the question in different ways, and just before she went home I asked her, "Mary, do you think we're a blue family or a green family?"

I guess that did it. Mary snapped. She answered me with an authoritative voice that kind of scared me. "Sweetie, you make a decision about this carpet right now and be done with it! This has gone too far. I think we should pray."

Mary so shocked me that I blurted out the word *blue*, and the decision was made in a nanosecond.

Mary started praying to the Lord about the blue carpet. I didn't even know she was a Christian. As she prayed, the volume and tempo increased until she was praying with such intensity I became uncomfortable. I even looked around to see if the neighbors were looking in the windows. I remember she was yelling out about God's important purposes—our moving and what would take place on our carpet, something like that. I don't remember what else she prayed, but I remember thinking she was way out there. After all, it's just carpet.

She was oblivious to me and my ignorant thoughts and contin-ued crying out to the Lord. Then her face lit up, and tears started streaming down her face. I perceived someone enter the room, and I instantly dropped to my knees on the floor beside her. Mary started talking to Jesus as if he were actually standing there. She started reminding him of all the things he had done for her and her family, and listed them, all the while crying. I felt like an intruder. Then she asked him to do the same things for my family. She scared me when she yelled out, really excited, "Thank you, Jesus!" like it was settled. She continued thanking him for what seemed like a long time. I didn't know there were that many ways to say thank you. When her grateful words turned into whispers of passionate love, my own emptiness and lack of passion for the Lord revealed itself and made me feel ashamed. Then Mary was quiet. Her sobs turned into sniffles, and she got up, walked to the closet, put on her coat, blew her nose, smiled at me with her huge smile, and walked out to her car.

I no longer had the desire or the energy to pick out any other carpet or flooring after my week of tiring indecisiveness. Burned-out, I ordered the blue carpet for the whole house, except the bathrooms and part of the kitchen. They gave us our installation date, and we could hardly wait.

Honey piled everyone in the car to go check out the newly installed carpet. We eagerly opened the front door of the farmhouse, and, lo and behold, the foyer and all the hallways were carpeted! The whole house was carpeted! I forgot to order tile for the foyer and hallways. I felt as though someone had kicked me in the stomach. *Why didn't I seek the Lord right away? Why?*

Honey and I looked down on the carpet in the foyer and noticed the muddy leaves we brought in. It hurt. Honey tried to comfort me by saying, "Just put some rugs down. If the hallways get too bad, we'll rip the carpet out."

It was moving day. I was directing the movers around the house when a woman came up to me with a plate of cookies. She said she lived nearby, and that our girls, Beth and Jill, had met on the school bus. It seems they decided that their mothers were exactly alike and that we should get together. After happily establishing that, yes, we were both crazy Christians, this woman dropped a bombshell in my ear, "I believe you're supposed to have a prayer meeting in your home." I survived the impact because I knew she couldn't be right! For one, I was still very much aware of my lack of passion for God after spending time with Mary. Plus, I was smack in the middle of moving. I couldn't think beyond that.

The girls were right. This woman and I became friends (life-long friends). But for the first month I knew her, this gracious lady drove me crazy about hosting a prayer meeting! I finally told her, "I'm sorry, Jean, but I'd never do something like that unless God himself told me to do it." Ahh . . . I was off the hook.

A few mornings later, I walked into our living room and turned on the TV, all the while wondering why; I never had the TV on in the day. Pat Robertson was talking. Then the camera moved in close to his face, and he said, "Is God asking you to open up your home for a prayer meeting? God is calling out people all over the nation to start prayer meetings in their homes." (This was in 1978.) I don't remember all he said, but I do remember, "If that's you, get down on your knees, because I want to pray for you." Of course, I went down on my knees, weeping, and received the prayer

A good number of women arrived at our house in a pouring rain-storm. Our meeting ended with everyone committing to come every

week to seek the Lord and to encourage each other. I was very excited about what God was going to do.

After they left, I noticed an identifiable path of soil coming from the front door into the long hallway to the living room and back down the hall to the kitchen and family room. Was I thanking the Lord for our prayer meeting and for the beautiful women who came? No. My mind was on the dirty carpet. Then I heard the voice of God (whether it was audible or spiritual, I don't know). He told me that I wouldn't have to worry about the carpet . . . and that we wouldn't be here that long. I was stunned, humbled, and experienced a hug of love and peace all wrapped together . . . a life-altering embrace.

Later I reflected, *God spoke to me! Unbelievable!* And then my mind said, *But it's about carpet? God speaks to me and it's about carpet? And we're leaving? We just got here and now we're leaving?*

It didn't make any sense, and I didn't tell a soul.

I pulled out my vacuum cleaner and vacuumed as usual, but something was different. The soil that had accumulated from the front and side doors into the rest of the house since moving day was gone. I remember just standing there and looking at the spotless carpet and wondering what had happened.

The prayer meetings continued once a week, and eventually another one at night, for all the years we lived on the farm. No matter what kind of traffic our carpet endured, it remained clean. If something was spilled on the carpet, I noticed the cloth would pick up the spill, but the carpet remained clean. We had multiple Christian gatherings, with hundreds of people walking in and out of the house; the carpet never soiled.

After one especially large Fourth of July picnic, with literally hundreds of people walking all over the grounds and then walking all through the house, our family was dumbfounded—the carpet was still spotless. How could this be? The carpet in our foyer, hall-way, and stairway looked exactly like the least-used carpet in the house. It all looked new.

I didn't understand the full revelation of our unsullied carpet until we started bringing the orphan lambs into the house. Then it dawned on me . . . the lambs were brought into the Master's home (heaven), their eternal inheritance. Their inheritance had luxurious blue carpeting beyond the reach of change and decay. Why? Because their inheritance is imperishable, unsullied, and unfading; reserved in heaven for them until that final day, ready to be revealed and enjoyed by them for all eternity.

The carpeting throughout our house never perished, spoiled, or faded. And just as the Lord had said, we wouldn't have to worry about it, and we wouldn't be there that long. The Lord transplanted us across the state about the same time five of our six children had married and four had moved to different parts of Michigan and Colorado. Though our family is now all scattered, we all carry within us the invaluable and reassuring lessons we learned from the sheep. We discovered who we are (we really are like sheep), who owns us (Father God has adopted us), who takes care of us (Jesus our Shepherd), who gives us our spiritual life and power (the Spirit of God himself), and where we are going (an imperishable inheritance waiting for us in Heaven)!

The Lord often gives miraculous signs to accompany his Word to help his people believe. And that people is . . . you.

> Know that the LORD is God. It is he who made us, and we are his;
> we are his people, the sheep of his pasture. (Psalm 100:3)

NOTES

I've taken Scripture verses and commentaries from the *Life Application Study Bible, New International Version; The Message: New Testament, Psalms and Proverbs; The Amplified Bible;* and *The Thompson Chain Reference Bible, New International Version.*

"Orphan lambs or lambs in search of their mothers are butted by bully ewes. Broken ribs and necks along with dislocated necks frequently occur." This quote was taken from the *Shepherd* magazine, *A Guide for Sheep and Farm Life,* 31 no. 1 (January, 1986) 12.

The first article and drawings I saw on dystocia (lambing problems), was also from the *Shepherd* magazine. I can still remember how my heart pounded when I viewed for the first time drawings of a lamb in the normal birth position; I knew I was in over my head.

When the lamb is born, the shepherd is supposed to "snip, dip and clip the lamb at birth." I really wasn't sure what that meant! It came from an article in "The Sheep Shed" section of the *Countryside & Small Stock Journal. Countryside* was my favorite magazine, as it covered every aspect of country living. I loved their philosophy too. "A reverence for nature . . . for maximum personal self-reliance and creative leisure; a concern for family nurture and community cohesion; a belief that the primary reward of work should be well-being rather than money; a certain nostalgia for the . . . simplicities of the past and an anxiety about the technological and bureaucratic complexities of the present and the future; and a taste for the plain and functional. "*Countryside* calls its practitioners *homesteaders.* Their special features included not only The Sheep Shed, but The Cow Barn, The Goat Barn, The Horse Barn, The Poultry Yard, The Homestead Kitchen, and much more. I wouldn't have survived on that farm if it wasn't for *Countryside*!

When I talked about tacking an article with drawings of delivery problems and their solutions on the barn's bulletin board, I was talking about an article from the trade publication *Best of Sheep!* "A Top-Notch Veterinarian Looks at Lambing (Normal and Abnormal)" with "Tips for the Shepherd-Midwife," by Dr. Don E. Bailey, DVM. Printed with a big, black, scary font was the quote, "NORMAL LAMBING IS EXPLOSIVE, COMPARED TO CATTLE!" It did not comfort me one bit! But this article and many others from this publication proved to be invaluable sources of knowledge as I walked on this journey.

The majority of facts I learned about breeding came from the *SID Sheepman's Production Handbook*, 2nd ed. (repr., 1981). This manual comes from the Sheep Industry Development Program, Inc., based in Denver, Colorado, in cooperation with the American Sheep Producers Council, Inc. It was from this manual, I learned how to make the nasty foot bath solution for the disease foot rot. I also viewed the grotesque photos of advanced foot rot in the hooves of sheep.

The Lamb Education Center in Denver, Colorado, was a wonderful resource. They once sent me a box of cookbooks, *Lamb Around the World*, to give to my customers—without cost! "You've Never Cooked Lamb?" was the first title on page 1. It was perfect for my customers and me.

The magazine *Sheep!* saved me many, many times. They once printed "The Shepherd's Calendar." I made a copy of it and referred to it every year. It was everything a shepherd had to do *before lambing*. It started at sixty days before breeding, thirty days before breeding, fourteen days before (flushing!), and then breeding time. Then it continues thirty days after the ram is turned in and thirty days before lambing—ending on lambing day. It didn't include lambing season—that is another whole calendar! And I thought raising sheep was going to be a picnic!

Behind every picturesque scene of snow-white sheep grazing peacefully on bright green pastures, polka-dotted with greeting card daisies, is an unbelievable amount of backbreaking and muscle-building work!